The Entrepreneur's Journey

Seraf
Compass
Publications

Other Books by Hambleton Lord & Christopher Mirabile

Fundamentals of Angel Investing
A Guide to the Principles, Skills and Concepts Every Angel Investor Needs to Succeed

Angel Investing by the Numbers
Valuation, Capitalization, Portfolio Construction and Startup Economics

Leaders Wanted: Making Startup Deals Happen
Advanced Techniques in Deal Leadership and Due Diligence for Early Stage Investors

Guide, Advise and Inspire:
How Startup Boards Drive Growth and Exits
An Overview of the Principles, Skills and Concepts Every Early Stage Company Board Member Needs to Succeed

Venture Capital: A Practical Guide
A Guide to Fund Formation and Management

The Entrepreneur's Journey

Hambleton Lord
Christopher Mirabile
Joseph Mandato

Seraf
Compass
Publications

Table of Contents

What Difference Does Timing Make?

Will Your Company Be Bought or Sold?

Introduction

"The glass is half full… and the other half was delicious"
Quotation seen on the side of a Jucy camper van

"What are the main ingredients for success with a startup company?" That's a question I hear all the time. There's no easy answer to this question, nor should anyone expect there to be. However, if I had to pick one of the most important ingredients in startup success, it would most certainly include the qualities of the company founder and leader. Founders are special people.

Creating and running a successful company is hard, laborious work with very little glamor and a lot of risk. It is hard because you constantly have to make bet-the-company decisions quickly in an environment of imperfect information. That can lead to a lot of angst and uncertainty. It takes a certain kind of person to see through the early growing pains, along with managing the daily ups and downs resident in a startup, and achieve success. Ultimately, this is a book about those people and the consequences and lessons that flowed from their decisions.

A few weeks before I took pen to paper to begin writing this book, I was visiting Great Barrier Island off the coast of Auckland, New Zealand. In the tiny coastal village of Port Fitzroy, I saw a bright green and purple Jucy camper van with the quotation "The glass is half full… and the other half was delicious" painted on the side of the van. My initial, quick reaction was to laugh at Jucy's clever witticism. In addition to the vibrant colors on their rental vans, they are well known in New Zealand and Australia for the cheeky expressions painted on the sides of their vehicles.

After a good laugh to start the day, I headed off with my family on a four hour hike to the top of the 600 meter summit of Mt. Hobson. While taking in the beautiful views on a gorgeous southern hemisphere summer day, my thoughts wandered back to that clever quotation. As the hike progressed, I came to the realization that this quip was a simple way to express what it takes to be a great entrepreneur.

It's common knowledge that entrepreneurs need to be optimistic. I don't know how any pessimist could ever overcome the barriers that startups regularly face. So, the first half of the Jucy quip ("The glass is half full...") is a classic way of describing an optimist. Entrepreneurs always see the glass as half full.

But what about the second part of the quip? ("and the other half was delicious") How do these words relate to an entrepreneur? During the most grueling steep section of Mt. Hobson, I thought about my years as a startup founder. I was always optimistic the company I was with would succeed. That optimism kept me going day-in and day-out. But, it was the journey from initial product concept, to building the product, to making the first customer sale, to scaling the business that really got me juiced (pun intended)! Sure, there were challenges and setbacks from time to time, but to me, living the life of a startup entrepreneur is "delicious."

In my experience, and in the hundreds of conversations I've had over the years with other successful entrepreneurs, it's the love and passion for what we do on a daily basis that keeps us going. It boils down to a question of temperament. If you don't find the long journey building a company to be "delicious," you probably shouldn't start a company.

Over the past six years, my business partner Christopher Mirabile and I wrote and published five books and eight course guides on investing in early stage companies. We gathered the material for these books from courses we developed over many years of working with startups and a lot of lessons learned from those experiences. We teach these courses to investors both at our angel group, Launchpad Venture Group, and to investors and entrepreneurs in classrooms all over the world. The course discussions led to much rich conversation, many additional insights, and much continued learning and refinement. Our instinct is to distill and capture. We are motivated to collect, organize and share those lessons. Joe Mandato, our co-author, shares the same motivations accumulated over his many years as a writer, teacher and investor.

Until now, the books we published and articles we authored were principally written as a series of educational guides for investors and entrepreneurs. Our main goal with the content is to teach versus entertain, and we expect our readers to treat those books, articles and course guides as desk references.

The goal this time around is different. With this book our intent is to enlighten and provoke thought in an entertaining and engaging way. Startup founders are special because their job requires constant difficult decision making. We want to take a look at the consequences and lessons flowing from those decisions. We try to capture the nuances and atmosphere around those lessons to convey more of the rich tapestry of the startup world.

This book is built around a fascinating collection of entrepreneurial stories. We hope our readers will keep this book on their bedside table to provide some entertaining stories that teach some of the most important startup lessons we've learned over the years. Stories have the power to make underlying lessons come alive for the audience. Understanding the core concepts in these stories helps both investors and entrepreneurs when they reach key inflection points with their companies.

Although we expect this book to be of most interest to investors and entrepreneurs, we purposely wrote it to appeal to a wider audience of people curious about the global startup phenomenon. Even if you aren't involved in the startup world, you will learn what that world is about and how entrepreneurs approach many of the successful and fatal decisions they make. We know their adventures will make for an engaging read.

To help with the readability of this book, we made a decision to have one principal voice appear to be the book narrator. From the reader's perspective, Ham Lord will narrate. That said, Christopher Mirabile and Joe Mandato wrote significant portions of the book, and we are all equal in our weight of authorship. So I can't take credit for everything you read. In addition, we reached out to many of our contacts throughout the startup world to provide our readers with quotations to highlight the stories. We can't thank them enough for recounting to us their own version of the entrepreneur's journey.

Joe, Christopher and I have an interesting viewpoint on the world of startups. The three of us combined were founders, senior management team members, or board members with over three dozen early stage companies throughout our careers. The majority of these companies either went public or were acquired. So we witnessed what real success looks like from the inside. And, yes, a few of our companies did go out of business, so we also had plenty of opportunity to swallow the bitter pill of failure.

In addition to the companies where we were actively involved, we have been investors in well over 100 tech and life science companies. With that large a portfolio of investments, we have an amazing perch to oversee a lot of stories unfold and witness a whole host of good, bad and ugly decisions by management teams. Each of us stored away a veritable vault of tales as we stood witness to the trials and tribulations of building a successful company.

If some of the stories in this book sound familiar it's because we incorporated elements of a few of them in our previous books. And, we use some of the underlying lessons in classes we teach at Babson, Stanford, Harvard, Tufts, University of San Francisco, MIT, Boston College, and Boston University. All of the stories in the book are based on real companies and real people. In one instance, the identity of an investor was changed because of a requirement to protect their privacy.

There are all sorts of startup companies launching throughout the world every year. Some startups are high-growth companies financed by angel investors and VCs, and others are traditional companies bootstrapped by the founders. Some are in slow growing market sectors, and others are in rapidly expanding, new markets. Some are local or regional companies, others are global. Some companies are in low tech service industries, and others are building high tech products. This book is not intended to tell the story of every kind of startup. Not all startups are designed for hyper growth and suitable for risk equity investment.

In this book, we plan to focus on stories relating to companies that we are intimately involved with. For us, that means those high-growth companies that receive financing in the form of risk equity from angel investors and/or venture capitalists. The businesses are going after mid-to-large market opportunities on a global scale. And, these companies tend to focus on either technology or the life sciences.

In a typical year, more than 500,000 companies launch in the United States. Of those companies, at most 40,000 are suitable for risk equity and fit our criteria for this book. That's less than 10% of all startups in the US. If you apply the filter which venture capitalists use on startups, fewer than 4,000 companies launched per year meet their investment criteria. So VCs find less than 1% of US startups to be in their wheelhouse.

One of the biggest challenges we faced when discussing what stories to include in this book was the breadth of topics that are key to the success and failure in the startup world. If we chose to cover all of the lessons we learned throughout the years, we would never finish this book. There would be a risk of losing the forest for the trees.

Ultimately, the winnowing-down process was not difficult. If you spend enough time around startups, certain themes continue to reappear over and over. We focused our study on the most universal issues. We felt these themes are some of the most important drivers of successful outcomes with early stage companies for both the investors and the entrepreneurs.

1) Who Cares About Your Product?
2) Should You Bet on the Jockey or the Horse?
3) Does Smart Money Invest in Bits or Atoms?
4) What Difference Does Timing Make?
5) Will Your Company Be Bought or Sold?

So for all of you who are optimistic and find great joy in taking on long, difficult challenges, welcome to the world of entrepreneurship. We have lots of stories to help you on your journey. And, for those of you who don't fit the entrepreneurial mold, sit back and enjoy some interesting tales of startup success and failure.

Theme One

Who Cares About Your Product?

"The aim of marketing is to know and understand the customer so well the product or service fits him and sells itself."

Peter Drucker

Chapter One

———————

Searching for Product-Market Fit

My favorite time of year in New England is early Fall. The heat and humidity of summer are gone, and the air is crisp and clear. Separating the cities of Boston and Cambridge, the Charles River is alive with sailors from several local universities and the Community Boating center. People jogging, biking, walking and enjoying the best of what Boston has to offer fill the sidewalks along the river. It was on just such an October evening in 1999 that I walked along the river mesmerized by the sparkling water and the Boston skyline. I was making my way to an entrepreneurship event at the Massachusetts Institute of Technology, better known as MIT.

About a year earlier, I left Advanced Visual Systems, my most recent startup. After a welcome break from the intensity of helping build a thriving company, I was looking to re-engage with the local tech community. MIT, recognized as a hub for innovation and entrepreneurship, hosts hundreds of tech events open to the public every year. Thinking back on that October evening, I was certain I would hear some provocative presenters speaking my favorite language, entrepreneurship.

Leaving the banks of the Charles River, I walked down Massachusetts Avenue to the main entrance of MIT. Like most universities looking to impress visitors with an architectural flourish, MIT's main entrance has an unusual feature called the "Infinite Corridor". This corridor is an 825 foot long hallway connecting several of the main buildings on MIT's central campus. Twice a year, the direction of the sun's rays aligns perfectly parallel with this hallway. The sun fills the corridor with light from end-to-end, resulting in a mini celebration of the university's own "MIThenge".

As I walked along the Infinite Corridor, I looked for signs to Room 10-250, the location for an evening event. MIT is well known for its somewhat nerdy approach to things. The naming convention for classrooms, offices and buildings is no exception. So, as you would expect, on the second floor of Building 10 you will find Room 10-250. The room is an especially easy lecture hall to find since it's located under MIT's iconic dome.

As I arrived outside the room, the hallway was abuzz with activity. Hundreds of would be entrepreneurs, students, and faculty were writing their names onto badges, and then making their way into the lecture hall. Finding a seat near the back of the room, I settled in for my introduction to MIT Enterprise Forum 10-250. Yes, the event was actually named "10-250" after the room it was held in… a perfect example of MIT logic at work.

Several MIT alums, looking to help colleagues and friends with challenges faced starting new companies, founded the MIT Enterprise Forum (the Forum) in 1978. Today, the Forum has twenty eight chapters located all over the world. And, in their words, their mission is:

"We inform, connect, and coach technology entrepreneurs—enabling them to rapidly transform ideas into world-changing companies. We are a global network of local organizations, inspired by MIT, and open to the world."

The Forum is just one of many organizations launched at the university focused on helping entrepreneurs build successful companies. Arguably, MIT is the most prolific university in the world when it relates to entrepreneurship. Naming successful companies with an MIT affiliation is, of course, far too long to list, but some of the more recognizable names include storied brands familiar to most: Bose, Zipcar, Dropbox, Hewlett Packard, Raytheon and Qualcomm.

Back in 1999, many considered the Forum's 10-250 meetings to be the premier events held by the organization. At a typical meeting, two companies would present their business plans to a small panel of local venture capitalists (VCs) and industry experts. The companies were young businesses. Most had a product on the market and some early revenues. After a fifteen to twenty minute pitch, the panelists would provide feedback to the entrepreneur. Once the panelists finished with their comments, the meeting opened up to feedback and questions from the audience. Sitting in on one of these 10-250 events was highly educational, much like sitting in on a case study lecture at a top business school.

What impressed me most was the constructive feedback delivered to the entrepreneur. Since the VCs weren't there to evaluate the company for an investment by their funds, they were willing to be very open and supportive with their comments. In other words, they told it like they saw it. Same with the audience. They were all there to learn, and when they could, give actionable guidance to the entrepreneur. That evening, I began my journey in learning how to listen to investor pitches, evaluate what I heard, and provide helpful commentary to the presenting team. I wasn't an angel investor just yet, but in another year I would be. The Forum helped me build the skills I would need to succeed in early stage investing.

On that October evening, there was an older gentleman sitting a few rows in front of me. He had the look of a retired MIT professor with his rumpled tweed jacket and disheveled hair. Halfway through the audience participation section of the meeting, he raised his hand to ask a question. His question went something like this:

"In the early days at your company, what percent of your company's resources did you apply to building a product and what percent did you apply to speaking to customers?"

Having spent time earlier in my career in a product management role, I immediately understood the significance of his question. Experience has taught me that too many entrepreneurs come up with a solution to a problem only to find out the solution isn't interesting to the customer. If you don't invest significant time in the early days of your business learning your customers' needs and desires, you are most likely doomed to fail.

For example, before Christopher Mirabile and I hired a single engineer to build our portfolio management platform, Seraf, we spoke to dozens of potential customers. And, since we would use Seraf to help us manage our own investments, we brought deep personal insight to the challenges faced by our target customer base.

By getting out of the office and meeting with prospective customers, we discovered the answers to two very important questions all companies need to know before they embark on the costly path of product development and product sales. First, what core capabilities does your product 'need to have' before customers are willing to use the product? Second, how much are they willing to pay for your product? Our in-field market research served us well in guiding us to the answers we needed before we launched our product development efforts.

In answer to the question posed by the Forum audience member, the entrepreneur rambled on for several minutes about how complex his product was to build, and why he had to apply most of his resources on the engineering team. Yes, he agreed, talking to customers was important, but he felt customers often don't really know what they need.

I remember the rumpled academic's constructive response to the company founder. "I believe you have it backwards. In the early days, you should spend double your resources on speaking with customers and understanding their needs versus what you spend on building your product. Put yourself in their shoes so you will have a better idea of their top priorities."

And there lies the heart of one of the biggest problems faced by startups... most people aren't interested in your product. Too many entrepreneurs go off in a misguided way to spend, or worse, collect and then spend precious resources building something very intricate and elegant that no one is asking for.

One of the biggest challenges faced in the startup world is "Finding Product-Market Fit (PMF)." To achieve PMF you need a very strong and unique value proposition for a very specific customer. Marginal savings on a marginal cost is not enough to get customers to leave their good enough and familiar solutions. You need to find real customer pain for your product to be a priority with a large segment of customers.

Success in the world of startup companies is elusive, and can take repeated efforts. In this theme we explore the stories of two companies who eventually get it right after multiple attempts trying to meet the needs of their target customer. And we recount the journeys of two companies for whom success remained just out of reach.

Over the next few years, I returned to MIT on a monthly basis to sit in on the Forum meetings. My newfound colleague, the rumpled academic, was frequently in the audience. He never once failed to ask his question about talking to customers. The audience never tired of his coaching the entrepreneur to get out of the office and spend more time speaking to prospects. And, I will never forget the important reminder he gave me: you must understand your customer.

Chapter Two

Are You Talking to the Right Customer?

In the fall of 1998, Joe Mandato led an MBA class through a case study. The case was on a medical device company Joe grew to a successful exit using a novel go-to-market strategy. The lecture was in Professor Thomas Hellman's Entrepreneurial Management class at Stanford University's Graduate School of Business (GSB), located on the east side of Stanford's beautiful, palm studded campus. The Spanish missionary style buildings of the business school were teeming that day with some of the best and brightest business students from all over the world.

Lecturing from the well-lit center of the deep auditorium-style classroom, Joe looked out on a gathering of sharp, young future business leaders. As is customary in business schools with guest lecturers, each student had their name displayed on a large folded card in front of them. The name cards reflected the broad gender and cultural diversity long a part of the culture that is the Stanford GSB.

Stanford was one of the few elite institutions with an early appreciation of the importance of entrepreneurship. It was no coincidence that experienced industry vets like Joe ended up in Stanford's classrooms to talk about real world case studies. In the years immediately following World War II, Stanford's provost, well known inventor Frederick Terman, staked the University's future on the development of new technologies. The expectation was these technologies might lead to new local companies and a thriving local ecosystem. Terman's vision ultimately manifested itself, years later, in what is today Silicon Valley.

After Joe's lecture, two second year MBA students, Zia Chishti and Kelsey Worth, approached Joe to ask his opinion of an idea they were developing. It involved a radically different approach to orthodontics. Like most entrepreneurs, they believed they had a disruptive idea, which, if successful, could turn a large industry upside down. It was born of the founders' own direct experience wearing metal braces. They remembered the pain of that experience and the unsightly look of metal braces, especially as young adults. The students proposed to replace metal braces with clear plastic aligners. Their company was to be named Invisalign.

Joe immediately saw the potential of their idea. He said, "Having had experience in this industry, I recognized the potential impact of their approach. I also knew reducing it to practice would be a significant technical and professional challenge."

Zia and Kelsey, while bright and ambitious, had no direct experience in orthodontics or in building a company. In addition to the many traditional company-building challenges, their product concept was going to require mastery of computer modeling, materials science, and complex manufacturing. Zia spent the first part of his brief career in consulting and investment banking. He had limited direct experience with the startup world, but he brought an optimist's enthusiasm to the challenge.

Kelsey, a bright and accomplished environmentalist turned investment banker, was more of a realist and brought a dose of practicality to the founding team. Joe Breeland, Invisalign's first VP of Sales, said, "Kelsey was a stabilizing force and her voice was one of reason, which was critical to the company at times."

Recalling those days, Kelsey said "I am just not a traditionalist. My father was always running for re-election, so I went to bed at night not knowing if he would have a job the next day. And yet, life went on. Entering Stanford I had no further interest in investment banking or consulting. I wanted something different, something exciting. Zia was a great salesperson and smart. He had the technical savvy to pull this off and it made so much sense. I was naïve, but I had the awful experience of metal braces. There had to be a better way. I believed this was going to be a big opportunity."

Given the breadth and depth of the challenge to get the company off the ground, Kelsey and Zia knew they needed a lot of help. Kelsey said, "The challenge was going from a scan to an actual device. Building the product, it had never been done before. Initially, the cost of building the product was outrageous and not sustainable if this was to be a successful business. Complicating things, the builder of the stereo lithography equipment we used went out of business in the middle of product development. So we bought his remaining inventory of seven machines."

The technical issues around materials science, the biomechanics of moving teeth, and sophisticated manufacturing were all challenging. From a business perspective, they needed help on how best to position the product, launch it, and drive adoption in this competitive market. They were going to need to raise substantial capital to execute their plan.

Joe Mandato became involved with Invisalign as an advisor, board member and investor. His primary question centered around whether the market would accept this disruptive new technology. As Joe considered the company's challenges, he said, "The biggest question for me was, could this team disrupt the large, conservative orthodontics market by addressing shortfalls of current practice and existing products?" Was this product solving a problem traditional products could not? How likely was it that customers would care about what these young founders were doing?

All entrepreneurs face a significant natural resistance relating to market acceptance and product-market fit when introducing a new product. This is especially true with a clinician-driven, go-to-market strategy, where there are multiple natural barriers to the adoption of innovation. First, a company introducing a new product needs to have data from laboratory testing and real patients that show the new product is safe and effective. To provide definitive answers to these questions takes time and money.

A second barrier is asking a clinician, i.e. an orthodontist, to change how she does her job, a skill and experience-based occupation requiring years of specialized education and training. New technology can involve uncomfortable changes in practice, and overcoming one of the most formidable types of inertia, the ingrained habit. If it can be shown there are clear benefits for the practice and patients, clinicians will eventually change their thinking. Showing clear benefits takes time and money. Fred Moll, the father of surgical robotics, said, "Market receptivity for disruptive technology evolves from abject horror to swift denunciation followed by begrudging acceptance." And so it was for Invisalign.

Medical products must also pass regulatory scrutiny. They must meet the high standards for safety and effectiveness set by the Food and Drug Administration. This regulatory process can be long and expensive.

However, a critical challenge facing every entrepreneur is finding the right customers. The metal brace technology of today was essentially the same as when it was first popularized in the early 1900s. The Invisalign product is a radically new approach. The product is a clear, plastic tooth aligner which is slipped over the upper or lower teeth to put gentle straightening pressure on teeth. It addressed a number of perceived shortfalls in the products produced by the manufacturers of traditional metal braces, including 3M, Sybron and Dentsply.

Invisalign's devices were practically invisible, a potential game changer in terms of aesthetics. Metal braces are painful and perceived by most as unattractive. Both Zia and Kelsey experienced this personally. Their product was designed to be more comfortable and take less time to straighten teeth. Patients could remove the device to brush their teeth for better hygiene.

But clear benefits for the end user customer are not enough. The product also had to work for the orthodontists. There was reason for hope. New products give early adopting clinicians a chance to be seen as technology-savvy practitioners. With the hope of shorter treatment times, the clinicians could grow their patient base, complete more cases, and make more money. And clinicians could expand their market to include people who needed orthodontics but would not wear metal braces.

To help drive market receptivity and to find the right customers, the company looked to early adopter clinicians willing to overlook product shortcomings to be among the first to try something new and exciting. By successfully targeting early adopters, traditionally estimated to be approximately 3% of most markets, a company can build credibility and revenues. Testing product-market fit was a critical objective when Invisalign approached the early adopter segment.

Invisalign's first vice president of marketing, Ken Varga, developed test markets in Austin and San Diego. The company needed real data to help them select customers to go after. Unfortunately, the test was too small and the results were inconclusive. Because they did not do a large and systematic test, they did not get the clear cut information they needed. But they got some hints. Ken said, "The data coming out of that effort demonstrated the easier the case, the higher the potential of a satisfactory outcome."

Based on the product's potential, combined with the anecdotal feedback, Invisalign was able to raise enough capital to refine the product and build a team which included an experienced sales force. In addition to a lack of understanding about which customers to target, the company did not have adequate product efficacy data. At best, they had a somewhat informed hunch the right customers were patients with simple teeth crowding cases and early adopter clinicians looking to differentiate their practice. Leadership, however, pushed to launch the product aggressively to a broad market. To drive market awareness and stimulate consumer and clinician demand, the company launched an expensive direct-to-consumer (DTC) marketing strategy.

It was a disaster. The DTC strategy was the wrong strategy at the wrong time. The campaign did not focus on the clinician, a serious error. It alienated a large portion of the orthodontist community by appealing directly to patients. And, instead of cost effectively testing a well-defined segment in a regional market, the company reached out to a national audience at great expense. This extravagant approach, across a   broad spectrum of poorly targeted media, delivered the wrong message to the wrong customers.

Joe Breeland, an experienced sales leader brought in to execute the sales strategy, cringes when recalling those early days. "If you happened to be watching your favorite cable channel after midnight," he said, "you were liable to see an Invisalign ad." Clinician reaction was universally negative. One told Jeff Tunnell, a regional sales leader to "Pack up your circus tent and get out of town."

Although it was still early in the product development process, the product performance issues were primarily due to poor patient selection. There was nothing fundamentally wrong with the product, but the early adopter clinicians used it across a broad range of patients. Disruptive products initially do not perform optimally in a broad market. Until its technology matured, Invisalign needed to target a subset of potential customers where they would have a higher probability of initial success. The test market was too small, the results unclear. It was clear however, clinician and patient expectations were not met.

After the botched launch and costly market learnings, the company eventually had enough information to identify its best initial target market. Joe Breeland said "We began to suspect the target market was made up of young professional women with a modest malocclusion." In plain terms, he continued, "It worked best for patients needing a modest correction. It was not data driven thinking, it was common sense. Until we optimized the product, we had to lower the market's expectations and our own. We also needed to re-establish credibility with our orthodontists."

The limited product effectiveness and profligate spending on poorly designed marketing tactics put a serious strain on the company. Kelsey said, "We didn't know how to watch our nickels and dimes. We spent money fast and not always wisely. Management was not as efficient as it needed to be, and often, there was no clear definition of who did what." The poor operating results spoke for themselves. The company consistently missed projections and faced the threat of running out of cash. They needed to change.

In 2002, the board of directors began a search to find a replacement for the company's CEO and co-founder. Given the complexity of positioning a hybrid clinical and consumer product successfully, the board was looking for a mature, sophisticated CEO with solid marketing chops. The search resulted in the appointment of Tom Prescott, a highly experienced executive, as CEO. Tom took several immediate steps to get the company back on its feet and to begin to accelerate its growth. First, he redefined and refocused his marketing efforts exclusively on the narrow segment which could benefit the most from the Invisalign product. Second, he invested heavily to improve product performance, thereby broadening its market.

Tom brought focus and operational competence to the entire team. He cut the cash burn to a manageable level. Tom said, "When I arrived at Invisalign, I found great promise in the opportunity, great people, groundbreaking technology, and an orthodontic market ripe for disruption by a clear aligner therapy. All in, there were many positives. Yet, the company lacked a culture which placed the customer and patient at the center of the strategy."

Prescott had to find and serve the people who cared about his product. The customer, he emphasized, was the clinician. He backed off the direct-to-consumer strategy. The Invisalign team implemented a plan to enhance the customer experience and develop closer relationships with a targeted and pre-qualified group of clinicians. To get to them and grab their attention, he said, "The team needed to refine and redirect the demand-creation marketing strategy and programs."

Tom asked his team two key questions. "Do our clinician customers really care about our product? Does it allow orthodontists to do something they could not do before? Yes! Using Invisalign, they can offer a therapy having much higher patient satisfaction with a core segment of customers who care primarily about better aesthetics." Further, the Invisalign product could provide a faster treatment regimen, less discomfort, and better hygiene for the patient.

Clinicians began to integrate Invisalign into their practice and use it for an expanding number of indications. The database of prescriptions grew, allowing the product to be refined and improved. This led to greater patient satisfaction, clinician confidence and an expanding market. The product's efficacy expanded beyond simple cases to moderate and certain complex cases. Invisalign finally found its way, and clinicians began to accelerate adoption of their technology.

Finding and properly targeting those early customer segments was the key to unlocking this large opportunity. With increased volume, product costs came under control and margins increased. With the improved targeting and marketing efficiency, the cost per lead went down because it was more relevant and therefore cost effective for the customers they reached.

Fast forward to today. Tom has retired, but not before growing the company's revenues to nearly $750 million. Knowing how to find customers who care meant the sky was the limit. The company has shipped more than one billion devices, seen annual revenues grow to $2 billion and maintains a large $23 billion market capitalization.

The stark contrast between Invisalign's early struggles and ultimate success stand as a powerful lesson on the importance of segmenting the market to find the right customers for your product. Until Invisalign figured out what it had, and for whom it was most relevant, it was a cash-consuming disaster-in-the-making. An unlimited marketing budget cannot help you if you are talking to the wrong people. But once you figure out your target market, the product begins to sell, sales and marketing efficiency improves, revenue grows, and the business succeeds.

Chapter Three

Are You Solving a Top Priority Problem?

Over the past twenty years, I've heard thousands of entrepreneurs present product ideas that will change the world in ways both small and large. In the end, only a tiny percent of these entrepreneurs are able to fulfill their vision for the product while meeting the customer's needs. What sounds like a great idea upon first blush often ends up on the scrap heap of failed ideas. "Why," you may ask, "does failure happen so frequently?"

There is no one answer to this question. In fact, entrepreneurs invent new ways to fail every day. However, there is one common theme I see over and over again in failed startups. Very few entrepreneurs truly understand their customers' needs and priorities. Founders rarely spend enough time getting to know their future customers. This lack of market knowledge almost always leads to a product that doesn't solve a critical problem for the customer. Such was the fate of Jim Keck and his company, SepSensor.

Born and raised in New York, Jim was an outstanding math and physics student. In 1944, while still an undergraduate at Cornell University, the US Army drafted Jim and assigned him to the Manhattan Project in Los Alamos to work on the first atomic bomb. Working closely with some of the most brilliant minds of his era, Jim developed the skills needed for a successful career in scientific research. During the immediate post war period, Jim completed his PhD in nuclear physics, and spent three years as a fellow at CalTech, followed by eight years in industry working on ballistic missile research. From 1963 until his retirement in 1989, Jim taught thermodynamics as a professor of engineering in the Mechanical Engineering department at MIT.

Jim's talents extended well beyond math and physics. His ever optimistic outlook on life, his enthusiastic personality, and his passion for designing and building eventually led him down the path to becoming an entrepreneur. One day, in the late 1990s, he was complaining to a friend about his septic system. Jim was frustrated by the frequency with which his septic system was pumped out by the local septic company. "How do they know when it's time to pump it out?" he asked his friend. "They can't tell how full it is since they don't have a way to visually inspect it."

Because of his thermodynamics research during his years at MIT, Jim knew how to measure the differences between liquids, solids and gases. So the question he asked himself that day was, "Can I develop a low cost sensor to tell whether it's time to pump out my septic tank?" Thus began Jim's journey as the founder of SepSensor.

Having spent most of his career as either a researcher or as an academic, Jim wasn't familiar with the process needed to launch and build a company. However, due to his past affiliation as a professor at MIT, Jim was able to take advantage of a free service at the university called the Venture Mentoring Service (VMS). By matching prospective entrepreneurs with skilled volunteer mentors, VMS provides practical advice and coaching needed by MIT affiliated entrepreneurs to get their businesses off the ground. One of Jim's VMS mentors was Erik Pedersen. Erik had a successful career as a software entrepreneur, and he provided Jim with critical advice needed to launch SepSensor. In addition, Erik was so enthusiastic about the company, he decided to join Jim as a co-founder and became the company's CFO.

Jim focused much of his energy in the early days at SepSensor designing and building the sensor so it could accurately measure and report the status of a residential septic tank. He focused the majority of his time and efforts on product development and very little on speaking to potential customers. Jim researched the potential competition to his sensor by checking at the patent office. As there was none, he patented his design. He felt the path to the market would be sales to each homeowner through retail establishments such as Home Depot.

As you can imagine, the sensor was located in a pretty tough environment, certainly not a place anyone would like to spend time. Jim had to solve this environmental problem, and he had to figure out a way to get the data from his sensor to the septic tank owner. Running wires from the sensor into the basement of the house where power was available was an acceptable solution. All of these engineering challenges took time to solve and increased the cost of building the device.

By 2003, Jim had built a working device and was getting ready to launch the product. But the company needed a CEO to help run the business. Jim might be a great inventor, but he knew he wasn't the right person to run the day-to-day operations of the business. Through his MIT connections, Erik introduced Jim to Mark Terrell. At the time, Mark was a seasoned executive with over thirty years experience building and selling instruments in a wide range of industries. His background and leadership skills were a perfect match for SepSensor. And, having both graduated with technical degrees from Cornell University, Mark and Jim had a lot in common from spending their undergraduate years in Upstate New York.

Before agreeing to sign on as CEO, Mark did a fair amount of market research to make up for the limited information Jim provided on the target customer. First, he looked into the potential size of the market. In the US, there are over 26 million homes with residential, on-site septic systems. He concluded that even a modestly priced system could result in a $1 billion dollar market opportunity. The general concept for the sensor and the pending patent on the device impressed Mark. But, he wanted to make sure there weren't any competing products or patents already on the market. So he researched the competition question, as well. Finding none, Mark viewed this as a good thing. He dove right in and became employee number three at SepSensor.

As an experienced CEO, Mark knew one of his first tasks was to undertake a thorough assessment of the market opportunity. According to Mark, "I wasn't going to make the common mistake so many entrepreneurs make by not talking to the customer and assessing whether we could achieve product-market fit." Mark realized selling through a retail channel was going to be difficult and expensive. In addition, after talking to a few potential homeowners, it was clear they didn't want to have anything to do with installing a sensor in their septic systems.

He started filling his calendar by meeting with executives at septic tank manufacturers along with owners of septic tank pumping companies. Within a short period of time, Mark started to get the lay of the land. "What I discovered was a fragmented market," said Mark. "Most pumpers were mom-and-pop operations with a small number of trucks covering their local territory. It was a low tech industry with limited interest in any sort of new technology."

Continuing his story, Mark said "I did find one septic tank pumper who found the idea behind SepSensor to be intriguing. I spent four months going over different business models with him. However, no matter what we did, we always ended up with the same result. Fewer pump outs meant less revenue for their septic business. If I was working so hard to get product-market fit, and was not developing a business model that makes money...hang it up. I knew it was time to cut our losses and pivot away from the residential septic tank market." Mark went from someone building a solution to a specific problem, to someone with a solution looking for a bigger problem to solve.

For an early stage company, pivoting away from your first idea can be a rough moment. Jim, Mark and Erik were discouraged, but they weren't ready to give up. Mark spent his days researching potential new markets for SepSensor. A short while later Mark relates, "While doing my research, I ran into another small company that built a sensor for the restaurant industry. Restaurant kitchens produce large amounts of grease, and most restaurants have a large-capacity underground tank called a grease interceptor. Just as with a residential septic system, the grease interceptors need regular pumping."

Mark discovered that pumping a restaurant grease interceptor is a fairly expensive proposition. Depending on the tank size, a pump out costs anywhere from $600 to a few thousand dollars. And, most restaurants play it safe and choose to have their tank pumped every three months, whether they need it or not. Furthermore, the last thing an owner wants is to shut down their restaurant due to a backup in the grease interceptor on a Friday night. That would be one expensive mistake. But, wouldn't it be better to know when and how often you need to pump the tank? To Mark that seemed to be a logical question to ask and answer.

Mark relayed his discovery to Jim. With some modifications, including moving to a wireless sensor that could relay data nightly via a cell phone connection, Jim's sensor could measure levels of grease solids and liquids. SepSensor embarked on a new journey to convince restaurant owners to use their sensor.

With a focus on the restaurant industry, Mark filled his days with meetings at restaurants. He met with restaurateurs who owned one or two restaurants. He met with owners of large chains. In the end, a decision was made to focus on chains. In theory, a single sale to a chain would result in deploying sensors in dozens or even hundreds of restaurants around the country. The price was set at approximately $1,000 to install the sensor at the restaurant, and then an annual service fee of $400. By eliminating one or two pump outs per year, a restaurant would save enough money to more than pay for the service contract. It was a win-win scenario… the restaurant saved money and SepSensor made money.

Mark found his first beachhead customer with Ruby Tuesday. With over 600 family restaurants in 43 states, Ruby Tuesday was an ideal customer to test out the SepSensor solution. During an initial trial at six different sites, SepSensor was able to cut the amount of grease interceptor pump outs in half. Ruby Tuesday was able to realize true cost savings shortly after installing the sensors. It looked like they had a potential success on their hands.

With this cost savings data from Ruby Tuesday in hand, Mark was able to convince an additional twenty restaurant chains to sign up for his service. The team at SepSensor was confident they found true product-market fit. According to Mark, "At the time, so many people told me this is a slam dunk. With over one million restaurants in the US alone, we were looking at a half billion dollar market opportunity. In the early days of SepSensor, we raised all of our funding from angel investors. Now, with some market traction, we were able to bring in investment from venture capitalists."

The market traction from a few forward-looking chains proved to be illusory for a number of reasons. Although Mark was able to sign up more than twenty restaurant chains, he ran into a number of unexpected operational challenges. First, the product was more difficult to build and install than originally projected. Mark said, "I knew I could use a manufacturing rule of thumb where you achieve price reductions on a product by building a greater quantity of the product. We found it extremely difficult to reduce the cost of each sensor unit down to less than $100. Without a lower price for our bill of materials, there was a serious negative impact on the projected capital requirements of our business."

Furthermore, SepSensor ran into issues when installing their sensors. "It's a lot harder than you might think to put a wireless sensor in an enclosed tank that needs to make a cell phone call every night from below a manhole cover in a parking lot," said Mark. "We found the solution by cutting a thin slot in the manhole side collar and into the restaurant's parking lot and then laying an antenna in the slot. However, when contractors grind the lot to resurface the parking areas, it would damage the antenna."

These product costs and installation issues were the least of Mark's worries. What really kept him up at night was how difficult it was to roll out the service after they convinced a restaurant chain to buy into the SepSensor program. Although chains might have a corporate office that manages the overall business operations, the restaurants each have varying local regulations and regulators have little concern that the operators save money. The facility manager might oversee multiple restaurants within a geographic territory. But, there are limits on their reach due to the need to convince local regulators to approve use of the sensor.

When a national restaurant chain signed up with SepSensor, Mark and his team had to reach out to dozens of local regulators across the US. This was a time consuming and frustrating process, and it resulted in an extremely slow rollout process for SepSensor's product.

These operational problems plagued the business, but in the end, it wasn't the cost of building the sensor, or the difficulty of installation, or the slow rollout process that resulted in the downfall of SepSensor. It was something less obvious to everyone involved at the company, including management, employees and the board of directors. This last problem came to light shortly after the Great Recession. As restaurant revenues dried up, restaurants focused on their front door, and cut many of the back office costs. Although SepSensor represented a cost savings for the restaurants, reducing the cost involved in properly maintaining a grease interceptor wasn't a top priority for the facility manager, or for anyone involved with the restaurant.

Yes, the cost savings were nice, but they weren't enough to move the needle. Saving a thousand dollars or so per year wasn't enough value to offset the time needed to oversee the service that SepSensor provided. It was easier to overpay for a pump out truck to show up every three months and get the job done. 'Just set it and forget it' … that's how most of us prefer to operate, particularly in fast paced businesses with a ton of other pressing daily problems like managing shifts and food inventory.

It turned out SepSensor had some product-market fit with a few early adopter customers, but the reality was they did not have a compelling enough value proposition to land and onboard customers in a sustainable way. The fact is, when they initially rolled out their solution, they did not truly understand their customers' business needs.

SepSensor shut down during the summer of 2012. Mark was able to find a home for the company's intellectual property. CiDRA Holdings, a product development company based in Wallingford, Connecticut, wanted to apply the core sensing technology into other industries. They purchased the SepSensor IP and hired Mark to oversee the building of sensors to increase the efficiency of copper mineral processing and paper production in large industrial plants.

Although the company was not commercially successful, Jim, Mark, Erik and the rest of the team at SepSensor undertook a big challenge and learned much along the way. What they learned about their market would have been more useful to know before they sunk so much time, financial capital and effort into a value proposition that just didn't have enough heft. Hopefully their story is a powerful reminder to all entrepreneurs of the importance of really understanding the customer and the customer's critical needs.

Chapter Four

People Don't Like Change

George Baker was a mid-fifties, tenured economics professor at Harvard Business School when he spent a well deserved sabbatical at his home in Frenchboro Island, Maine. A beautiful place, with a ferry that only runs three days a week, it is infamous for the fog that gives living off coastal Maine numerous challenges. When the fog lifts, you can see Acadia National Park to the north, a smattering of additional rocky, green-fringed islands to the east, and the blue sparkling waters of the open Atlantic to the south. And to the southwest, George notes with pride, he can see the three blinking red lights atop a wind farm he helped develop on Vinalhaven Island, twenty miles away.

Previous to the installation of Vinalhaven's wind farm, it had always been a mystery to George as to why there was no wind generation on the Maine coast. This was despite an electricity cost about three times the national average, and near constant wind availability. George said, "I had this house out here on the island. I was on the board of the little cooperative electric company serving this island and several others. As time went by, I got interested in energy issues, and particularly renewables." He decided he would devote his sabbatical time and business skills to solving the mystery.

The answer, as George came to understand, was a clash between local culture and standard project financing practices. George said, "Lots of developers approached people on the islands of Maine and said, 'Hey, let us build a wind farm here. We'll build it, and we'll own it, and we'll sell you the power.' And these crusty Maine types said, 'No, this is our island. We need to own the project.' Project backers could not get past that. The islanders were unwilling to allow outsiders to come in and own these installations."

Understanding that reality, George set out on a journey that would become a career turning point. "I started working on this problem and figured out a way to do it with community ownership, and still be able to take advantage of all of the federal and state subsidies for renewables. It was tricky. It was novel." Using George's financing approach, the Vinalhaven Island wind farm project eventually got off the ground.

With his sabbatical at an end, George found himself back in his office at Harvard Business School wondering what to do next. George said, "Into my office walks this bold, MIT-trained mathematician named Jessica Millar. She said, 'I hear you have a wind project on an island. You must have a grid balancing problem. I have a technology that could help you.'"

George started talking to Jessica about her idea, and became fascinated. Their conversation was a deep dive into how regional and national electric grids are managed. Orthodoxy at the time was to cycle on-and-off large electricity generating plants (coal, nuclear, natural gas) as needed to keep the grid supply in balance with fluctuating grid demand. Jessica explained as power needs changed with the growing adoption of solar and electric cars, this approach to managing the grid was not going to work for much longer.

With Jessica's help, George quickly grasped the looming problem. Due to the accelerating growth of many smaller and much less predictable sources of renewable power, such as solar and wind installations, energy grids were going to have big and unpredictable supply fluctuations. With an   increase in electric cars there were also going to be more demands on the grid. In theory, large batteries could be used to soak up extra power in times of surplus, and release power in times of high demand. But commercial scale grid storage batteries were still too expensive to deploy at scale. Jessica explained the modern electrical grid was certain to have major difficulty properly integrating renewables.

Controlling and balancing renewable supply fluctuations from a small number of massive wind farms was challenging enough. It became overwhelming when combined with thousands of residential rooftop solar installations. More complicated yet were emerging ideas like distributed micro storage. This is a radical idea of using many small batteries, such as the batteries of electric cars in people's garages, to help stabilize the grid.

Electric grid operators are, as George puts it, "able to twiddle a few knobs" to ramp up and down a small number of large, traditional fossil fuel and nuclear power plants. Jessica got George wondering "Who's going to twiddle the knob on 50 million batteries in people's garages? The control room is not going to have 50 million little individual knobs." It was clear to George, as it had been to Jessica, that the world was going to need an entirely new decision architecture for the electric grid.

Jessica explained to George that she had designed just such a new decision architecture. She built a sophisticated algorithm that could balance a grid by switching many individual devices on and off. She further explained that grid operators were in desperate need of this kind of service. Better yet, she enthused, her system could deliver cost savings to the electricity user. Her algorithm pulled in a variety of data, both historical and forecasted, to predict low-cost/low-demand periods and high-cost/high-demand periods. This could allow users of connected devices to access much lower time-of-use electricity pricing.

George saw immense commercial value in her concept. However, as he recalls "Jessica needed help to start a business. She is completely brilliant. She is one of the most extraordinary minds I have ever known. But when she dove into the details of this topic, she was almost incomprehensible."

George agreed to help write a business plan for Jessica's startup, which she called VCharge, so it could raise some initial money to test out the idea. Because George earned much goodwill and many connections from the wind farm, the seed financing came quickly. Maybe too quickly, considering the dangers that can come with overconfidence.

The business plan was not simple. Under the plan, the company would be paid to provide grid balancing services to regional electric grid operators. Demand management was an essential part of grid balancing that kept the demand for electricity on the grid in balance with the available supply. In order to provide that demand management, George and Jessica knew they had to adjust load on the grid by remotely switching devices on and off. To achieve meaningful impact on something as large as a regional grid would require a huge number of devices they could turn on and off. Scale was the key to making their new grid decision architecture valuable. To provide valuable grid services, they needed control over enough electricity demand to have an impact.

How would this generate revenue for their company? Regional grid operators would pay for this service because it generated significant operating cost savings. Without balancing services, whenever demand spiked, the grid operator would pay power plants to ramp up and down. If VCharge could help by temporarily reducing demand until the spike passed, the grid operator could avoid paying generators for these grid regulation services. They would share the savings with VCharge.

George and Jessica's business plan had a second potential revenue stream. At times of high demand, electricity is most expensive. Their ability to control the timing of demand would allow them to supply electricity for their customers at times when electricity was particularly cheap.

There was one major wrinkle. Electricity demand is directly correlated with productive work. People use electricity for a reason. Factories cannot be turned on and off at will. For their plan to work, George and Jessica knew they were going to have to find a large amount of electrical devices they could turn on and off at will. The challenge was finding devices that could be switched off without affecting the user of the device. For that to work, the device needed to be associated with some kind of on-for-a-while, off-for-a-while duty cycle. That meant some kind of storage or temporary buffer allowing it to cycle off without impacting the user.

They looked at all sorts of electricity uses, from industrial air compression (you run the compressor until the air tank is full of pressure, and then you use the air until the pressure drops and you need to run the compressor again) to ice rink refrigeration (you chill the rink down and then shut off the system until it warms back up to a critical point). But every category of use they considered was either too small or too difficult to wire for remote control. Or it came with demanding commercial users who would be very unlikely to cede control of their vital electricity supply to a startup.

Their eureka moment came with the discovery of residential electric thermal storage heaters. These simple devices are essentially a large box of bricks with heating elements woven in amongst the bricks. The devices run heating elements until the bricks get hot. The tremendous thermal mass of the bricks allows them to slowly give off steady heat to warm the home for several hours. Not only did these heaters represent the perfect buffered, intermittent energy demand, they were residential, rather than industrial users. There were a fair number of them, and George and Jessica assumed the supply of these storage heaters could be increased at any time through increased deployment.

George and Jessica got to work. They found an engineer who could design a prototype heater control unit. They made an informal deal with Concord Municipal Light Plant in Concord, Massachusetts to test their grid services solution on some local thermal storage units. No sooner had they started than they realized a few hundred thousand dollars in seed money was not going to allow them to deploy a meaningful amount of heater control units. It was clear they were going to have to raise additional money from investors. That would require finding more potential load than one small town in New England could provide.

Jessica's research led her to a large collection of electric thermal storage heaters in northeast Pennsylvania. The heaters had originally been pushed by the local utility as an experimental means for increasing electric load to soak up some of the huge capacity of the local Three Mile Island nuclear power facility. Now, decades later, that same utility was hitting their customers with large rate increases. Most were angry and looking for a less expensive heating solution. Jessica and George felt they found their perfect test bed. So they were optimistic as they set out to raise $1.5 million to build the control units and get them installed onto the Pennsylvania heaters. Unbeknownst to them, it was going to prove nearly impossible to coordinate and combine meaningful load in Pennsylvania.

The investor funds came in, but two problems combined to make the rollout very difficult. The first problem was the engineering contractor who offered to build the control hardware for them. His time estimates were overly optimistic by a factor of four. He needed almost two years to complete the project instead of the six months he promised. The second problem, as George recounts, "By the time the hardware was ready, almost all of the customers with any kind of get up and go had already replaced their electric thermal storage units. There were a lot of units left, but all the people who might be early adopters for us already changed their heaters out. I can't tell you how many people we talked to who said 'I changed out my heater last year.' All said and done, we were never able to convert more than about twenty percent."

When reflecting on this challenge, George remains mystified why it was so hard to get people to adopt the technology. George said, "All we needed to do was go to people and say 'let us come in and do a modification to your heating system. We guarantee your heating system will work better than it did before, and you will get twenty five percent back on your electricity bill.' Electric heat in Pennsylvania at that time was at least a thousand bucks a year. So this is two hundred and fifty bucks a year that people are saving. And, because of our algorithm taking cold weather forecasts into consideration, your heating system will work better than it did before. We had testimonials from people who were wildly enthusiastic. Still, we had an extremely hard time getting people to adopt."

George takes pains to point out the technology was not the problem. "Our technology was really quite extraordinary. Every time we would go to see PJM (the regional power transmission organization) they would say 'We can't believe what you do. No one is doing this.' But we did not have scale. We never got above two megawatts. We figured in order to break even financially from our PJM contract, we were going to need at least ten megawatts."

The customer adoption friction with residential customers in Pennsylvania had beaten George and Jessica. It didn't look like there was any way they were going to reach the kind of scale they needed to break even with PJM. After striking out in Pennsylvania, they tried a similar program in Maine. They faced the same result, despite riding the coattails of a utility-sponsored subsidy for electric storage heaters. Just as with Pennsylvania, it was clear that no amount of effort could get people to switch Maine customers away from trusted oil heat.

This was a challenging time for the company and its founders. Money was running very low. They could not seem to overcome customer resistance, build load, and break even on a project. George and Jessica knew they had to find a better way. "So we started looking elsewhere. We needed a place where they didn't have cheap natural gas and where they had a lot of electric thermal storage heat. The place we found was England," said George. The company got an introduction to UK grid operator, National Grid. They were delighted when National Grid expressed keen interest in what VCharge was offering.

The market looked very promising to George and Jessica. George said, "There were five million homes in the UK with storage heat. Better yet, many of them were in what's called social housing or public housing. And we thought this is great. We don't have to convince individual homeowners. We can go in and retrofit their homes because the boss of their housing association wants to do it. And better still, in some fraction of these housing associations, heat was included in the rent. So the landlord has a bigger financial incentive."

George and Jessica felt sure they finally had a low friction market. "Excitement built." George said, "We negotiated a lucrative and innovative contract with National Grid to deliver a new type of grid service. We were using our advanced technology to lower bills and provide very advanced grid control. We developed a product that only we were going to be able to deliver. No one else could move fast enough and have enough control over their electric load. A standard generator couldn't possibly deliver that kind of control. We called it 'fast dynamic response.' And they agreed to pay us a lot of money for this control."

All VCharge had to do was walk right in and wire up the controls on all that storage capacity waiting to be aggregated. George said, "Our job was to combine and bundle up this load and get it up to 100 megawatts. We thought we could get up towards 500-1000 megawatts in the UK, and then we would have been wildly profitable."

Alas, George laments, "Once again, we thought we had the perfect place to roll out our service. In the UK, social housing was full of these old storage heaters that didn't work very well. But once again, adoption was astoundingly difficult." It turns out getting the bureaucratic people at the social housing authorities to agree to anything was almost impossible. They were essentially employees of the local boroughs. They had no incentive to do anything risky and rock the boat. It was outside of their job description.

George and Jessica hired an experienced sales person with a deep commitment to the mission. They tried as hard as they could to break through. But George said, "We never got there. In two years in the UK, we got just one full tower block installed. It was so slow. We didn't understand the difficulty of the process we were up against. We thought this was going to be a slam dunk. It seemed so clear it was the right strategy."

Before long, they were completely out of money. Rather than shut the company down, the VCharge board authorized one final bridge round of financing to fund the search for a buyer for the company. Ultimately, progressive energy provider OVO, the second largest independent energy provider in the UK, acquired the VCharge assets. There was enough to pay the company's creditors, but nothing left for the investors and other shareholders.

Asked to reflect on the product-market fit lessons gleaned from the VCharge experience, the business school professor in George Baker comes out. "Whatever you do, don't underestimate the friction in adoption." To grow quickly, a solution needs to be easily adopted and integrated by a customer. A business looking to introduce a new concept cannot assume massive behavior changes on the part of the customer. It is not consistent with human nature. Customers are generally afraid of disruption. George learned trying to convince consumers to change a perfectly good heating system, let alone to cede control of that vital utility to a small startup, was just asking too much. George sums it up well,

"People don't want to worry about stuff. They don't want to change things. It's easier to keep it the same."

For VCharge and its supporters, underestimating that friction, and failing to come up with a way around it, meant the company could never build control over enough electrical load to allow its brilliant technology and complex business model to shine. Today the VCharge brand and concept live on as a small part of OVO. VCharge was once a high-flier, intent on solving the global renewables integration problem. Its ambitious vision was to provide an entirely new decision architecture for the electric grid. It is now a greatly diminished shadow of itself, humbled by the immense forces of customer inertia.

Chapter Five

Make It Easy for Customers to Buy

Watching your family lose their home to entrepreneurial failure would scare a lot of people right into a conventional non-entrepreneurial career. Not Jon Strimling. The son of a semiconductor equipment entrepreneur, and the grandson and great grandson of entrepreneurs, he'd grown up around entrepreneurship as a way of life. Jon saw first hand the empowerment that comes with entrepreneurship.

Jon entered college just before his family was hit with financial ruin due to a financial setback of his father's. That experience was sobering in terms of the volatility of entrepreneurship, but Jon was not scared away. Jon viewed the setback as a challenge he needed to tackle. To him it was just a question of how cheaply he could live and how fast he could rack up academic course credits using his merit scholarship and part-time earnings before his modest college savings ran out. Jon lived in a fraternity because it was the cheapest rent he could find, and added as many extra courses as the registrar would allow. After a grueling sprint, he graduated with a degree in engineering in less than three years, including spending a year in the university's required work co-op program.

Jon did not immediately begin his work life as an entrepreneur. He had a fascination with manufacturing and wanted to get some experience first. After two years as an engineer at GE's aircraft engine division, Jon enrolled in MIT's *Leaders for Manufacturing Program*, an innovative dual degree program funded by some of the largest and best known companies in the world.

Given Jon's background in technology and operations, the MIT program led him to a role with an investment firm, American Industrial Partners. The firm placed him in multiple companies requiring help in operations and technology. First, Jon took a job implementing improved financial systems at the Sweetheart Cup Company, a manufacturer of paper cups. This was the first of three experiences with wood and paper related products. Then, Jon took a job leading the launch of synthetic extruded wine corks, a technology that now, twenty years later, is the dominant synthetic cork technology. After that, Jon worked at DEKA Research & Development, the Manchester, New Hampshire-based development lab of one of the country's best known entrepreneurs, Dean Kamen.

The work for Dean Kamen led to Jon's second experience with a wood fiber related product. Kamen asked Jon to explore commercial manufacturing feasibility for one of his research projects, a confidential and proprietary method for efficiently extracting energy from wood pulp. The need for inexpensive and renewable energy sources exposed Jon to the virtues of wood pellets. These manufactured fuel pellets stoked Jon's curiosity. After five years with DEKA, he left to take on a senior growth and development role at New England Wood Pellet.

It was at this point, after a few experiences as an employee, that Jon's entrepreneurial drive came to the forefront. After some research, planning and discussions with NE Wood Pellet's CEO, Jon worked to create and spin out an independent eCommerce sales and distribution company that could drive distribution of the manufacturer's pellet output. As the founder and CEO of

WoodPellets.com in 2006, Jon gained valuable entrepreneurial chops, including raising venture capital and private equity, and experiencing his first startup success. Things got tough during the financial crisis in 2008, but Jon righted the ship and, after a good six year run, stepped away from the company in 2012.

A third wood fiber-related business soon came knocking. Because of the decline in US newspaper circulation, an installer of cellulose insulation in Maine began to worry about the diminishing supply and increasing cost of recycled newsprint. As the production and recycling of newsprint steadily dwindled, the insulation industry that flourished by recycling newsprint into building insulation was in trouble. Raw material costs were going up, and quality was going down. The quality drop was due to single stream recycling which put more impurities from other materials into the paper waste stream. This was giving the cellulose manufacturers cost and supply headaches and giving the insulation installers big problems with cost, dust and clogged machines.

This local installer, in collaboration with the University of Maine, hired a research team to see if they could find a solution. Before long, their research zeroed in on cardboard. Unlike newsprint, recycled cardboard was a substance whose supply was growing daily due to the growth of eCommerce. So, if they could find a way to make insulation out of cardboard, their supply problems would be solved.

After a good deal of experimentation, the research team figured out how to use a pulping process to break down recycled corrugated cardboard to replace some or all of the newsprint with cardboard fibers. The installer and his colleagues had formed a predecessor business to commercialize the technology, but they were unable to get any funding or commercial traction. Seeking someone to lead their efforts with fundraising and commercialization experience, the team was referred to Jon as a potential CEO. Jon soon formed a new commercial company called CleanFiber to commercialize the idea.

When Jon was asked to take a look at CleanFiber, his first reaction was to roll his eyes and think, "Oh, no, not another wood pulp company." His preference was to expand into a new area with new opportunities for learning. But the match with his skills and experience along with the market opportunity were just too good to ignore. Jon said, "There weren't a lot of professionals who had rapidly grown companies in the wood fiber industry."

Jon dug in and, based on his early research, quickly became bullish on the opportunity. The first question in his mind was would the market accept this cardboard based product? "I did diligence on the technology, and I did diligence on the market," Jon said. "The first call I made was to the largest buyer of insulation in the country. I talked to an executive there I had known for ten years about cellulose insulation. They wanted to build a plant in the Northeast themselves but couldn't due to a shortage of paper. At that time, I did not tell him about the cardboard idea, but I said I had the fiber aspect covered. He said if I can get fiber and make an equivalent quality product, I should build the plant and he would order millions worth of product from me. This was how my first diligence call went."

Shortly after that call, Jon made a less encouraging discovery. Preliminary research told him he could deliver an equivalent product, and do it for a better price. But when he attended an industry conference to research competitors, he realized the CleanFiber founders and research team at the University of Maine had over estimated the cost advantage built into their original plan. This was a crushing blow, and Jon had to think long and hard about whether the business was even viable.

Jon knew production costs had huge implications for both the customer and the company itself. With higher costs and lower margins, the company's capital needs were going to be higher, and the financial returns on invested capital much less attractive. This meant Jon would have difficulty raising needed financing to build his company. Perhaps more importantly, without the ability to price aggressively, achieving customer adoption was going to be much tougher.

Jon knew the importance of speed. "Rapid customer adoption was the whole ball game in building a growth oriented business. Even when things are going well, they take longer than you expect. But if there's any kind of friction in adoption, you can double the timelines. If our product is easy for people to adopt, if it solved the problem immediately for them, that was going to allow us to build the company much more quickly than if we did something more complicated. I've always said you can build a business from one 'if' but not two," said Jon.

Recognizing from the outset he had to make it a no brainer for customers to buy his product, Jon said, "We had to be equal to or better than the competition on literally every metric. Because if you are, there can be no objection. For example, since our product is superior, in theory we should get a higher price for it. Our investors ask why we don't price our product with a premium to the competition? And my answer is it's all about the speed of adoption. As soon as you put any hurdle in front of a customer, they can bellyache. 'Oh well, you're five cents higher than the other guy.' If the customer is bellyaching, you're going to slow down your sales process dramatically."

Once he recognized the cost problem in his business model, Jon immediately pulled out of investor meetings and put fundraising on hold. But, he was not ready to give up on the company. By then he'd had significant career experience wringing cost and inefficiency out of manufacturing operations. He thought he might be able to find some improvements. And he knew he'd gotten through some lean times as a scrappy college student, so he figured he could get through this as well. Jon said to his team, "Even though we're not financially attractive to investors today, we are eligible for some good grant opportunities while we see if we can further develop the technology to be fundable."

It took two long years of very lean living and taking other work to pay the bills. Eventually they found enough manufacturing, operational and supply chain savings to not only get back to cost parity, but to give them a meaningful cost advantage. "I built a business model and negotiated agreements with suppliers that gave us operating cost leverage. We also improved capital efficiency by leveraging equipment that other people already owned. And that made a huge difference in the business," Jon recalled with pride.

Achieving cost parity was a big win, but Jon knew cost parity wasn't the only customer objection he had to overcome. His experience taught him product-market fit was about more than just price. He knew his business model had to be a fit for the customer as well. In Jon's experience, you have to meet customers on their terms. "With product-market fit you think about every facet of the business. We tried to structure supply agreements with our suppliers that look exactly like the way the supplier is dealing with every other customer of theirs," Jon said. "Everywhere we could we took out friction. The fit isn't just about the product. It's about the business model. If we can deal with them in the manner they used to deal with their suppliers, that's better."

Product design was a focus as well. Jon recognized the importance of good design in finding the product-market fit. And by design it is more than how the product looks. It is how the product works. At first thought, one might assume there is not much scope to change the design of a standard dimension, 25-pound bale of cellulose insulation. But Jon and his team spent months interviewing customers to understand their frustrations with the existing products. He knew he had the competition beat on dust and machine clogging. But by listening to the customer, he learned of another huge opportunity to design and deliver a better fit.

"To date we've done well over 100 customer interviews," said Jon. "But early in the process, after maybe 40 or 50 interviews, we discovered the packaging was very important to installers. They're very frustrated when they buy from the competition. Our customers have a guy in the truck, and he throws the product down to a guy in the driveway. And when they inevitably burst open, they have a mess on their hands. Product-market fit is about talking to people who go onsite and seeing what's actually happening. We realized, wow, the bag isn't just a label. It's part of the product that has an important function in the field. And so we're using better bags than most of the competition because it matters to the customer. We want to take as much hassle out of buying from us as possible."

Careful attention to solving the customers' problems and knocking down barriers to adoption, means fast and friction free customer adoption. Jon said, "So when a customer adopts us, all of a sudden the bags don't break, their hoses don't clog, and their equipment doesn't need to be cleaned out multiple times during a shift. And all of a sudden they are not dealing with dust. They're paying the same amount to cover more square feet than they can with our competitors' products. It becomes an absolute no brainer. If you want to scale a business rapidly, then the challenge is how do you get to the point where it's an absolute no brainer like this? You want the sale to be that easy."

Customer psychology also plays a role. Part of what makes Jon good at finding product-market fit is his natural empathy for the customer. He makes sure to avoid highlighting that Clean-Fiber was a new player in the market. "If you look at our website it doesn't say anything about a new product. We're not advertising new products because of that reason. And we are paying attention to the color of our cellulose. We could have launched a cardboard brown cellulose. But we take care to make sure ours is gray because everybody else's product is gray. We didn't want to do something that looked markedly different than what was out there," Jon said.

Customer psychology involves more than product and marketing. Treating customers respectfully and allowing them to root for you can play a big role in generating customer loyalty. People want to give their business to the vendors they like and enjoy doing business with.

Jon understood this from the start and took pains to relate to his customers. "Cost is a factor, but hassle and the emotional response of the customer matters too," said Jon. "When you take the hassle out of people's lives, they notice and appreciate you. The difference between CleanFiber and the competition is we're much more responsive. Sure, we are lower cost, but we use some of our cost advantage to be higher touch. We offer customer support in an industry where most people try and automate everything. This approach builds customer loyalty by building relationships with customers. And in today's world that's so rare it got us a lot of attention and loyalty."

This focus on customer psychology can be extended to how you sell the product. In CleanFiber's case, Jon experimented with getting out and cold calling customers on job sites. "At times we showed up with a pallet of product and tossed bags to them out of the back of a rented truck," said Jon. "They're thrilled with us because we have a personable sales rep who is working with them and explaining what we do. Something like this never happened to them before. We ask them if they want to check our product out, and of course they say yes. So we hand them bags of products. People respond because it's so different than getting the 47th email from some random company. They respond to the respect and the outreach."

From operations, to design, to marketing, to sales and customer support, Jon relentlessly engineered friction out of the customer adoption process. Is it possible to precisely quantify the impact of reduced friction in the process? Probably not, but it is clear in the case of CleanFiber it played a hugely important role in the company's early traction and ultimate success. Jon's instincts and the efforts he took should serve as a lesson to other founders. No matter what you sell, you should look for ways to make the customer comfortable with your product, you should allow them to buy in familiar ways, and your distribution should work the way they are used to. It's a physical constant. Friction slows things down. Remove friction for your customers and your business will grow as fast as Jon's bales fly off the trucks.

Theme Two

Should You Bet on the Jockey or the Horse?

"The pessimist complains about the wind. The optimist expects it to change. The leader adjusts the sails."

John Maxwell

"Great leaders communicate a vision that captures the imagination and fires the hearts and minds of those around them."

Joseph B. Wirthlin

"The supreme quality for leadership is unquestionably integrity. Without it, no real success is possible, no matter whether it is on a section gang, a football field, in an army, or in an office."

Dwight D. Eisenhower

Chapter Six

———

You Know Great Leadership When You See It

What defines a leader? Titles can help identify possible leaders. Validation, however, certainty requires seeing a leader in action. Joe Mandato has held many leadership titles and been in many leadership roles. He'll leave the quality of that leadership to others to ponder. What he does know is that he was not born a leader. Nor did he learn leadership in college or graduate school, despite the leadership classes he took and the conscious efforts he made to build his leadership skills.

Joe learned leadership by watching it in action. Looking back on his long and varied career, Joe tells me as he gained experience, he not only changed as a person but grew as a prospective leader. Along the way he had the good fortune of meeting some powerful leaders he both admired and respected. To their credit, and to Joe's good fortune, several were great teachers. He grew and developed his approach to leadership by listening carefully, and more importantly, by paying attention to what they did as they went about their business. When I asked Joe to give me an example of how he learned from great leaders, he told me the following story.

"We all benefit from good luck at some point in our careers. My good luck and opportunity to learn came early. It was almost as if fate conspired to throw me into close proximity to a great leader and a wonderful man when I was still a very young and impressionable professional. For more than four years, I lived right in the vortex of his leadership approach. Looking back I know I didn't fully appreciate it at the time, but the opportunity to observe great leadership and internalize its key components and style had a profound and lasting impact on my life. Now that I am in the later stages of my career, I realize the lessons I learned during those early years were very formative. I have no doubt they have been a key driver of my success. Those lessons are especially valuable today in my work with entrepreneurs building teams and developing their leadership skills."

Joe continues his story, "In 1968, I received a draft notice inviting me to prepare to serve in the U.S Army. I beat the local draft board to the punch and joined as an enlisted person, which gave me an opportunity to choose my Military Occupational Specialty (MOS). I chose a healthcare related MOS. After basic infantry training, a demeaning experience at best, I headed to Fort Sam Houston in San Antonio to learn my specialty as a medic and as a social work and psychology specialist. I completed the course and received orders to head straight to the Republic of Vietnam."

As Joe packed his gear and prepared to return home for a short 'goodbye' leave before shipping out, an officer from Army personnel called him in for a meeting. To his great surprise, they ordered Joe to head to officer basic school, and more importantly, discard his orders to Vietnam. To this day, Joe has no idea where those orders came from. He said, "I have no clue how or why this happened, but hey, I accepted the offer, signed up, completed officer basic training, received my commission, and traveled to my first assignment, the Pentagon in Washington."

Wearing a brand new, freshly pressed uniform, Joe headed to Washington, D.C. and the Pentagon. Like most new arrivals, Joe found it to be the most imposing, complex and confusing building he'd ever experienced. Once he found his way through the maze of highly polished floors and concentric corridors, he reported to his commanding officer, an affable career Army "lifer" with the rank of lieutenant colonel. Before Joe could even sit down, the lieutenant colonel said, "Do not unpack your gear, you are going to Walter Reed Army Medical Center, way north of where you are standing. You will interview for a posting with its new commanding officer Brigadier General Carl W. Hughes." What Joe didn't know at that moment was this assignment would change his life forever.

All new general officers, such as Brigadier General Hughes, are entitled to a so-called Aide-de-Camp, a right hand person and an officer who, on behalf of the general, does it all. Off Joe went to Walter Reed, a 1000 bed general hospital with little idea what he was getting into. The second-in-command interviewed Joe and he passed muster. Next up was an interview with General Hughes, which according to Joe, seemed to go well. Before Joe could process what had happened, Colonel Prettyman let him know he got the job, and so began the experience of a lifetime.

To this day, Joe wonders what they saw in him, a young, inexperienced and freshly-minted officer. He had neither attended a military academy nor had any experience in the requirements of the job. Nevertheless, he reported to work early his first morning as the Aide-de-Camp of the commanding general of this high-visibility, premier military hospital. When he arrived, the general was already there. Joe inquired of the general's executive assistant as to the general's start time, confirming as he suspected that it was very early indeed. The next day and every day thereafter, Joe arrived fifteen minutes before the general. That simple habit proved so effective, that even now, fifty years later, Joe is first to his office, and views the establishment of this habit as an early but key step in his journey as a successful leader.

After a short time tending to his desk, General Hughes began each day by rushing out in a blur wearing his physician's white coat, not his dress uniform, replete with stars and lots of ribbons.

Upon seeing this, Joe ran to Anne, his assistant, and asked where the boss was going. Anne said, "He walks the hospital each day. He greets and visits with staff and patients, especially those wounded in Vietnam, and whatever VIPs were at Walter Reed for treatment." It was the General's walkabout.

Years later when Joe read Peters and Waterman's book, *In Search of Excellence*, he smiled knowingly when the authors cited one of the components of excellent leadership as "management by walking around." General Hughes had clearly figured that out on his own and practiced his version of that theory religiously.

On his second day at Walter Reed, Joe asked to join the General for his daily walkabout. The General agreed. Always eager to learn, Joe was smart enough to bring a pen and paper with him whenever he walked the halls with General Hughes. His diligence was richly rewarded. These walkabouts provided the opportunity to meet all manner of leaders from the president himself and members of his cabinet, to leaders of Congress, foreign dignitaries and senior military staff. Joe still has a photo from the front page of the *New York Times*, which shows the President, his military aide, General Hughes, and cropped from the left side of the photo, Joe swears, is young Lieutenant Mandato.

Joe was fortunate to attend meetings with the General's senior officers as they managed the day-to-day activities of this large military medical institution. From this enviable position, Joe had a front row seat to watch great leadership at work. Reflecting on it over the years, Joe recognized that the General possessed key leadership traits, particularly those in the realm of "EQ" or high emotional intelligence.

General Hughes took note of what people said, questioned them at length and more often than not, accepted their recommendations. Never once, in Joe's presence did he raise his voice or dress down his team. The General showed great humility. Even though he rose to the highest ranks of the Army and was decorated with medals and ribbons, he wore his white physician coat while in the medical center, not his formal uniform with stars and other indicators of his standing.

The General also seemed to intuitively understand how important it was for a leader repeatedly to communicate a clear vision and maintain a constant focus on the underlying goals. He left no doubt in the minds of anyone in the organization where the organization was headed and why. He made clear that everyone was there to serve the men and women of the U.S. Military. His daily walkabouts demonstrated this humility and focus on the mission. He was respectful of his people, always curious, always learning.

Not surprisingly, the General's high EQ and great leadership skills meant he attracted the most competent people around him. While Joe may have been too young to appreciate the full measure of their true competence, he certainly noticed the General's team always seemed to get a lot done, on time, and in a manner which met the general's high expectations.

Perhaps more important than any of his leadership characteristics, General Hughes was a man of great integrity. Although he was kind and respectful, he was always truthful and direct in his words and his deeds. He engendered trust by letting everyone know where they stood with him at all times. He kept his promises and honored his word. As a result, his team admired him, learned from him, trusted him, and embraced him fully as their leader. Given the timeframe, General Hughes was quietly building a culture focused on trust and mission first.

Looking back on it now, Joe realizes having the good fortune to be in close professional proximity to such a leader was a life-changing opportunity. For Joe's development as a professional and a leader it was a formative experience. Joe learned very much from him and to this day he emulates this great man for who he was and how he led. And he applies these lessons daily in working with young entrepreneurs and their startups.

The book you are reading today is all about building new and successful enterprises. All three of the authors believe great leadership and competent teams are critically important predictors of probable success. We are not alone in that belief. Research at Harvard Business School clearly demonstrates that institutional investors are more likely to invest in a great leader and team than a great product. Paul Gompers, who conducted some of this research, said "Investors attribute more of the likelihood of ultimate investment success or failure to the team than to the business." A great entrepreneur and a great leader often share the common trait of self-awareness. In knowing oneself, you are more liable to fill gaps in your skills with a talented team, and in doing so, enhance the probability of success.

From our collective years of diverse experiences, we watched great leaders emerge, observing the styles and behaviors of those with whom we worked. And, by reading academic research, we learned the impact of leaders and great teams on driving business success. In this theme we will look at several different approaches to leadership taken by a number of successful entrepreneurs. These leaders were of varying ages, working in different kinds of companies and across numerous industries. They all, however, had certain things in common. They were tenacious, intelligent and had high integrity, and they pulled together a strong team of board members from whom they could seek help and support in order to effectively lead their companies.

Chapter Seven

One Plus One Equals Three

The story of Adam Martel, Rich Palmer and their startup named Gravyty is a story about great leadership. These two relatively young founders created and succeeded with a completely new category of product in a difficult and conservative market. They overcame the odds and did so with leadership and talent. And, they would not have been given the chance to do so had investors not spotted those leadership skills.

Investors in startup companies experience so many successes and failures over time that they cannot help but evolve their way of thinking about the drivers behind those outcomes. As drivers go, the importance of leadership is recognized universally. So most investors think a lot about the quality of a company's leaders. Christopher, Joe and I are no different. Experience taught us there are certain traits that are very important in startup founders, particularly in startup CEOs. We always look for those traits of great leadership. If we don't see them in satisfactory measure, we tend to move on without making an investment, regardless of the idea.

The most important trait in our hierarchy of leadership qualities is integrity. This is our shorthand for honesty and forthrightness, transparency and openness. Given how much judgment and discretion is vested in startup leaders by their investors, it stands to reason you would be looking for someone you implicitly trust with your money.

Perhaps second most important is something we refer to as tenacity. To us, this term means determination, doggedness, resilience, perspective, even stubbornness. Startups are really hard. Success is improbable and at times seemingly unachievable. We need to see signs that a startup leader will push through the obstacles with the perspective that nothing worth doing is ever easy.

The final element in our top three attributes is a combination of IQ and EQ. This equates to basic intelligence combined with emotional intelligence. The value of basic intelligence should require little explanation. It takes smart people to solve tricky problems. Getting a startup to succeed can be one of the trickier problems around.

The importance of emotional intelligence is less obvious, but no less consequential. By emotional intelligence we mean people skills and communication skills, both speaking and listening. Things like the ability to motivate people, the ability to sell, the ability to influence, the ability to read people, the ability to partner effectively, the ability to evaluate and hire good people, and the ability to know your own limitations and manage your own emotions.

These are all skills that are required in abundance when leading a startup. Startups usually have limited resources. Progress requires getting the most you can out of each team member. That requires creating an environment where a group of high performing individuals can meld into a high performing team.

The final two items we look for seem, on the surface, unrelated, but they share one common aspect. Both can be overdone. One is knowledge of the target market and the other is leadership charisma.

Market knowledge is important because you need to understand the dynamics of the market you are going after including the competitive landscape and what the customers want or need. Coming into a startup already knowing some of that can save time and resources. However, it can also be limiting. That is why it is called *conventional* thinking. Not every opportunity calls for a conventional approach. Sometimes what is needed is to think differently. How can we totally disrupt a market or create an entirely new market? In cases like that, deep market knowledge can limit creativity by grounding a founder too much in conventional thinking. Sometimes what you need is someone new enough to a market that they don't realize what they are trying to do is impossible, or at least not care that it is unconventional.

Similarly, leadership charisma is something that is very valuable, but it too can be overdone. You want someone who can walk into a room and command everyone's attention. Someone who is comfortable in the spotlight at least part of the time. Someone whose passion is infectious and whose example inspires others to follow. These are the pied piper like attributes of great leaders. They inspire others to take up their cause.

But this charisma can be taken too far. Coming across as too slick or salesy can turn people off. Telling people only what they want to hear goes beyond EQ into the realm of being a phony. Investors don't want someone who is always being a cheerleader. They want substance as well. They want someone who knows when it is time to make a speech and when it is time to listen. They want someone who is as interested in the question as they are in shooting off a fast answer. It is a fine line between a charismatic leader and a snake-oil salesperson. But if an investor knows to look for that line, and listens to their instincts, they can generally sense when someone has crossed over it.

In concert with these five attributes, we also find it very helpful to evaluate potential leaders through the lens of temperament. By temperament we mean someone's natural inclination along the extroversion/introversion spectrum. Neither inclination is more valuable or desirable than the other, but a person's natural temperament affects their fitness for different kinds of roles. In our experience, finding a work role that fits your natural temperament is almost always a precursor to finding long-term sustainable fit, happiness and success.

What makes temperament so fascinating in the context of startup leadership is leadership requires skills associated with each end of the temperamental spectrum. Things like deep analytical thinking, charting your own course, being a visionary, taking the time to develop the deep technical mastery needed to be an inventor, being less interested in norms and more willing to be unconventional, are all things you associate with startup leaders, and also with introversion.

Being good at selling, working well with other people, being charismatic and comfortable in the spotlight, and having a high resistance to sales rejection are also things you associate with startup leaders. But they come from the opposite end of the temperament spectrum. People capable of adroitly and comfortably covering that entire range don't grow on trees. People like that are special and fairly remarkable. What can often happen is two founders working closely together form a unit which allows them to cover the entire temperament span.

This is exactly what happened in the case of Adam Martel and Rich Palmer. They founded Gravyty in 2015 to make non-profit fundraising personnel more effective and efficient. These relatively young founders not only embody all of the five attributes we look for in startup leaders, but together they combine to bring capabilities that cover the entire temperamental spectrum. This allowed them to form a tight bond as a founding team, and in turn, jointly drive their software startup through fast growth and toward a very successful early exit.

Adam was born in Andover, Massachusetts. As a young person he changed schools frequently as his parents took every opportunity to switch him to a better school whenever they could. He credits this constant need to readjust for some of his people skills and his competitive drive. Adam's father was an entrepreneur and his mother worked in an administrative role at a local college so that Adam could attend college tuition-free. Adam's first job out of college was as an investment manager at State Street Bank. After two years he switched to working as a fundraiser in higher education. The desire for an MBA led to a job as a fundraiser at Babson College where he could utilize Babson's free tuition plan for employees.

Adam met Rich in Babson's MBA program. Rich had grown up in the western Connecticut town of New Fairfield. When he arrived at Rensselaer Polytechnic Institute as a freshman, Rich was the first in his nuclear family to enroll in a bachelor's degree program. Rich graduated RPI with coding skills and spent his early career moving between New York City, the San Francisco Bay area, and Boston. He worked as a product manager and as a co-founder of a web and mobile development company. After a three-year stint managing a group building very advanced quantitative analytics tools at Relationship Science on Wall Street, Rich decided to round out his business education by pursuing an MBA at Babson.

Rich said, "The idea for Gravyty was born when Adam and I became friends and decided to team up on an entrepreneurial venture. After working on some different concepts, we settled on the idea of Gravyty and then honed it as part of an MBA class project. The concept was to combine my skill set in machine learning and analytics with Adam's skill set in fundraising. We were going to build a software tool to help frontline fundraisers figure out how to prioritize their target lists and raise money more effectively."

Adam and Rich enjoyed working with each other. As they developed the idea, they became convinced it was commercially viable. They decided to launch the idea as a real company before Adam even finished his MBA. As the more extroverted of the two, Adam took the CEO role. Rich was more technical and introverted, so he took the President and CTO role.

Christopher met Adam and Rich early in their fundraising process and was immediately impressed by them. Since he lives close to the Babson campus he said, "I offered the only slot I had which was to stop by campus very early in the morning before my day began. Neither founder blinked at the suggestion of a sunrise meeting."

Christopher's preliminary sense going into the meeting was that they were targeting a very difficult market. His initial enthusiasm was limited. He recalls, however, "Adam and Rich had so much earnest enthusiasm. They displayed so much passion and thoughtful candidness as they answered questions. I began to sense that I was in the presence of a special team." He decided on the spot to help them out by getting them connected to other investors in his network for advice and feedback.

I was one of the investors Christopher introduced to Gravyty. Over the ensuing months, Christopher and I began to meet regularly with Adam and Rich. We were both struck by their lack of artifice as well as their intelligence and high EQ. They had thought deeply about the opportunity, but they were honest about needing help. They never pretended they knew something they didn't. They communicated and listened well, and implemented the advice they were given. They were different temperamentally, but worked extremely well together, often saying the same thing simultaneously or completing each other's sentences.

In the early days, most investor feedback was negative. There were concerns about the challenges of the target market, the strength of the product's value proposition, and the lack of any commercial traction to prove its viability. But Adam and Rich showed their tenacity and determination by refusing to take no for an answer. They doggedly educated investors on why the opportunity was real. Recalling that period, Adam said, "Everybody counted out this industry. All these biases stacked up against us. But Rich and I were raised to think like David vs. Goliath, fighting against something bigger. It's how we operate. It's when we are at our best."

They also used their EQ to listen carefully for the concern behind the question and make sure an investor's underlying anxiety was addressed. One memorable episode flowed out of their first big pitch to a large group of investors. Although naturally extroverted, Adam was nervous because he did not have a lot of experience pitching to a large group. He had some natural charisma, but he did not have it dialed in perfectly yet. He did a solid job with his presentation.

He garnered enough investor interest to move into due diligence, but there were still some skeptics lurking. One was a former university president who stood up after the pitch and offered a very pessimistic comment. In her view, universities would never buy this. Adam and Rich were crestfallen, and rightfully worried that this viewpoint would sink their due diligence chances. But they did not give up or shy away from the criticism. They called the investor and asked if they could have a few minutes of her time. After more than an hour of discussion in her living room, she came to realize that some of her assumptions about the product were wrong. Adam said, "I'll never forget it. When we walked her through the story, she agreed with every point. She just didn't realize what they added up to. She had a sudden visceral reaction. She looked at me and said, 'This could actually work. I realize my fundraisers didn't have the technology they needed.' She turned 180 degrees from a skeptic to a supporter."

Gravyty made it through the diligence process and Adam and Rich raised their first financing with Launchpad leading the round and participating heavily. Christopher joined their board of directors and had a front row seat to watch and help them grow as leaders. Christopher said, "The way Adam and Rich ran Gravyty reflected their differences as individuals. They each had the EQ and self-awareness to know what they were good at and what they weren't."

Adam talked about it in terms of space, saying, "The first thing that we got right was being able to make space for each other. Rich and I have spent enough time talking to other founders to know that making space is one of the best indicators for whether they'll be successful or not. Rich lets me do what I'm best at, and allows me not to do what I'm not very good at. Knowing that, between the two of us, we have a more complete team than most other founders. We talk every morning, and I can't think of any decision that's taken longer than half an hour. We talk it through. Who's best to do this. Is that my skill set?"

Not everything was smooth, however. Both founders had to learn certain things about themselves. Adam's fierce competitive drive motivated many team members, but not all of them. Some could be overwhelmed by it. Adam had to learn from Rich that there were different ways to tap into different people's motivations. Not everyone saw everything as a competition. Rich had to learn from Adam that people did not always need multiple levels of detail in their instructions when he was delegating to them. Rich had to learn to be a little less trusting and a little more wary of being manipulated. They both had to learn to channel their innate people skills into hiring skills to allow them to build a first rate team.

They had a few hiccups along the way, but they learned from them and put together an amazing young team. Their basic instincts were remarkably good. They found themselves able to build a strong and winning culture. Rich's technical brilliance, attention to detail, and ability to focus on the customer's needs inspired the technical team to pivot the product from the initial dashboard concept to a far more advanced product incorporating artificial intelligence and natural language processing. The resulting tool not only tells fundraisers who to contact, but also does a first draft of the communication. Rich's drive for excellence and enterprise-level functionality was an inspiration to his team.

Adam's dogged determination was similarly inspirational to the sales team. One particular episode illustrates how Adam demonstrated tenacity to his team. Many of Gravyty's potential customers had their data locked in software made by a multi-billion dollar company in the industry. Gravyty needed permission to integrate with that company's software in order to win those potential customers. The CEO of the company repeatedly rebuffed email and telephone outreaches from Adam.

The situation became increasingly critical as Gravyty struggled to win new customers without a technical integration. Finally Adam decided enough is enough. He sent the CEO an email that said, "I'm flying to your city next week on Tuesday and I am going to sit myself down at the coffee shop across the street from your office all day. If you can't make fifteen minutes to come down and see me or invite me over, then the next day I am going to come over and knock on your door and sit in your lobby until you speak to me." Adam said, "The CEO took the meeting. That is how I do tenacity."

Adam and Rich grew the company quickly. Following the suggestion of Christopher and other investors, they focused on making contacts amongst other companies serving higher education and nonprofits. They went to industry and financial conferences and formed a high-profile council called the AI in Advancement Advisory Council (AAAC). Rich said, "The AAAC had the involvement of very senior people in the fundraising and higher education industries because it offered the chance to have open discussions about where artificial intelligence technology could impact fundraising." Eventually the AAAC raised Gravyty's profile high enough to attract the attention of several competitors and several private equity firms specialized in buying growth stage software companies.

Neither Rich nor Adam had ever been involved with selling a company. But, they were determined to get it right and worked closely with their board to optimize the outcome. The board stressed the importance of securing multiple bids in order to maximize the potential value of the company. Adam's competitive instincts and determination kicked in. He began accelerating discussions with the other potential buyers, which resulted in Gravyty receiving two term sheets and an expression of interest at the same time. Adam and Rich were constantly learning throughout the process. They showed a lot of professionalism and leadership skills in their determination to take care of all their stakeholders, from investors to employees to customers.

The acquisition of Gravyty closed in late 2019. The winning bidder was a large California-based private equity firm. Despite the fact that Gravyty was only three years old, the buyer ended up offering an extremely good valuation. Shareholders had the choice of selling all, some, or none of their stock for a valuation that represented a 10X multiple on the company's then-current revenue forecast. The buyer ended up owning about 60% of the company. Adam and Rich stayed in their roles and kept their Gravyty team intact. Investors were thrilled to have received some liquidity at a phenomenal return on their investment, and equally excited about the long-term potential of their remaining shares.

None of this would have been possible without the leadership provided by Adam and Rich. Although they were relatively inexperienced going into it, they represented a nearly perfect example of the traits we have learned to look for in leaders. They did not do it alone. They had the self-awareness to ask for help when they needed it. They pulled off a successful exit due to their integrity, their tenacity, their intellectual and emotional intelligence and their perfectly complementary temperaments. They have work to do to write the final chapters of the Gravyty success story. But as Christopher said, "They have reached one of the greatest milestones a startup leader can reach... having all your investors want first dibs on your next venture."

Chapter Eight

Knowing When Experience Counts

A wounded soldier, far from a trauma center, has a so-called golden hour to be treated for serious injury to maximize chances of survival. Surgical robotics initially were designed to treat these battlefield injuries as fast as possible, remotely. By remote, imagine the robot is in a location separate from the surgeon using it. The surgeon is in this second location performing the surgery. The robotic platform features arms positioned over the patient and surgical tools at the ends of each arm. A communications link connecting the surgeon to the platform allows her, while seeing an image of the patient on a screen, to manipulate surgical tools on the arms through a master hand device. The robot mimics the surgeon's exact hand movements to perform the surgery. First pioneered in the early 1990's, this futuristic technology is now available and used worldwide for multiple surgical applications requiring precision and consistency.

Intuitive Surgical was founded in 1995 by Dr. Fred Moll and Rob Younge. Its mission was to build and sell commercially feasible, sophisticated robotics for use in surgery. Today, the company is a powerful and enduring example of the impact competent leadership and a great team can have on a complex management challenge. Intuitive introduced robotic surgery to the lexicon of healthcare innovation. In the hands of a great leadership team, the company led the disruptive change robotics brought to the market. Intuitive established an entirely new product category and with it redefined the global practice of surgery.

Fred Moll is a medical device visionary. After graduating from the University of Washington Medical School, he began his surgical training, and developed an interest in small incision laparoscopic surgery. In this type of surgery, a camera is inserted through a small incision in the umbilicus. The camera visualizes the internal organs and allows surgical tools, inserted through small incisions, to perform surgery. Fred co-founded Endotherapeutics to develop those tools. After its acquisition by US Surgical, he co-founded Origin Medsystems to continue the pursuit of his vision for creating innovative small incision surgery tools and techniques. In time, his career path would take him to the emerging world of surgical robotics.

Intuitive's story began in 1994 when Fred paid a visit to the Stanford Research Institute (SRI), an independent research institute in Menlo Park, California. Fred met with SRI engineer Phil Green. Phil and his team, working with the Department of Defense, had prototyped sophisticated robotics technology to treat wounded soldiers remotely. Fred understood if surgical robots worked as intended, they could disrupt the conservative profession of surgery and create an entirely new category of sophisticated medical technology. This was the impetus for his meeting with Phil. Even then, Fred believed, "Robotics could become the future of how surgery is practiced."

Fred's visit to SRI was every bit as inspiring as he hoped it would be. He immediately wanted to apply Phil and his team's technology to non-military surgical applications. He believed robotics was a natural extension of minimally invasive surgery. He wondered if Origin, a cash and resource-strained startup at the time, could afford to take on the risk and cost of a robotics R&D project?

Fred knew a robotics project required focus, unique skills, and a long design and development process. Building a surgical robot is a complex challenge. It requires substantial capital to develop a working prototype and more capital to accommodate the slow adoption of new technologies in healthcare. After assessing the risks associated with these challenges, Origin's senior management decided it made the most sense to spin out a new company called Intuitive Surgical which would license the robotics technology from SRI.

Fred left his position at Origin Medsystems, and its parent Guidant, to be Intuitive's first CEO. Fred had a clear strategy in mind to launch and build the company. His ambitious goal for the future of surgery, and his aggressive plans for how to accomplish it, inspired and motivated potential employees and investors. He was able to gather a strong team around him. As a leader he also understood his own limitations. He said, "My value-add is pattern recognition focused on products." He knew professional investors needed more than just a product visionary in a founding team. They invest in teams with a mix of skills. In addition to the deep understanding of markets and products that Fred possessed, the company needed leaders with engineering, operations, manufacturing, finance, regulatory and marketing skills.

Fred started a search for a technical leader to help launch the company and raise the necessary financing. He sought the help of a leading healthcare investor, Mayfield Fund. Fred gained access to and support from two visionary physicians, Russell Hirsch, a Mayfield Partner, and John Freund, a Mayfield advisor, to find a world class technical lead. John introduced Fred to Rob Younge, an accomplished engineering and operations leader, and a proven entrepreneur. Rob was one of the co-founders of Acuson, a pioneer in the field of ultrasound imaging. Rob joined Intuitive as co-founder. This new, complex technical challenge and

Intuitive's ambitious mission excited Rob. He believed he had the technical chops to accomplish this herculean task.

With a co-founder at his side, Fred's next challenge was raising capital, a challenge compounded by the complexity of this disruptive robotics technology and the capital-intensive nature of what Intuitive was trying to do. Investors' market research showed Intuitive's total addressable market could be huge. Robotics was used successfully in industries requiring precise, repeatable functionality. Robotic surgery might offer clinical benefits over traditional open surgery. But, disruptive change does not come easily in healthcare. It usually takes time and significant capital to support the product development and the marketing necessary to win over industry key opinion leaders. Fred recalls early conversations with surgeons, "One expressed abject horror at the idea of robotics. He asked if I was out of my mind. Another surgeon said it would be criminal to use robotics."

The engagement of Russell Hirsch and John Freund at Mayfield Fund brought needed credibility to the company and its truly disruptive ideas. This credibility helped attract key new team members. Those team members, plus the robotics technology, which could redefine the practice of surgery, provoked lots of financing interest. Intuitive raised $5.5 million led by Mayfield Fund with participation from Sierra Ventures and several notable medical device industry veterans.

With cash in hand, the team set out to build the world's first commercial surgical robot, which they called DaVinci. They planned to prove the doubters wrong. The team developed a detailed operating plan. They hired key engineers including Dave Rosa, and built a working prototype to demonstrate the technology in an animal lab. Dave joined from Acuson. He said, "I had tremendous respect for Rob Younge, and Fred's vision blew me away."

Having built a working prototype, Fred and the team felt the company was ready to move out of the deeply technical phase.

They faced a critical decision. Given the scope of what the company was trying to do, they recognized the need to find a world class CEO. Changing leaders is always a pivotal decision, and with Intuitive it was made earlier than most young companies. Fred said, "If you're creative, you're usually not structured. I know I'm more on the creative end of the spectrum. We would need more structure." Fred's self-awareness and the willingness and alignment of the management team to find the right leader was a credit to the founders and proved critical to Intuitive's ultimate success.

With the decision made, the CEO search began. Three quality candidates meeting the position specifications were identified. After a rigorous bi-directional screening process, Intuitive hired Lonnie Smith as their CEO in May 1997. Mayfield's Russell Hirsch, also one of Intuitive's founding investors, added, "We looked for a mature, experienced executive who could mentor and lead a young team to achieve its ambitious goals. We saw that in Lonnie. We also saw an intellect that fit in with the smart Intuitive team."

Lonnie had broad and deep professional experience. He joined Intuitive from Hillenbrand Industries, a diversified Midwest manufacturing company. He had occupied positions of increasing responsibility over twenty years, the last as Senior Executive Vice President and board member. He did not, however, have experience at a venture-financed startup. Reflecting on Lonnie's early tenure at Intuitive, engineer Dave Rosa said, "Startup experience didn't matter. Lonnie was all about content and substance. Company size was unimportant. Our mission and our vision excited him."

Why was a seasoned executive like Lonnie interested in Intuitive? Lonnie said, "At the time I was interviewing for the CEO position at Intuitive, I was in discussions to join one of two successful billion dollar companies. During a call with my daughter, she asked where I was in my decision and I described my options. She said, 'Dad, why don't you do something that will make a difference?' She reset my decision criteria and priorities. I believed Intuitive could make a significant and lasting difference. I took a 70% pay cut and moved to California from a company with ten thousand employees to a company with twelve."

References confirmed Lonnie was a mature, credible, skilled and smart operating leader. Dave Rosa called him a great athlete. "He just seemed to do everything well and had a ton of experience doing it." The team was comfortable with Lonnie and confident he could lead the company as it transitioned from an R&D organization to an operating business. And Lonnie was determined to bring only enough structure to Intuitive's fast paced environment to get the job done, while allowing enough looseness to maintain its passion and excitement.

Given his experience, Lonnie understood the complexities of a capital equipment company. He set standards for effective capital deployment, inventory management, complex design processes, supply chains, and margins, all critical issues at Intuitive.

Operations were not Lonnie's only focus as a leader. Early in his tenure he initiated a process to define Intuitive's culture. From experience Lonnie understood the importance of having shared values, goals and practices in a company. He knew companies often neglect the process of defining their culture, and regrettably allow a default culture to develop on its own. Intuitive did not. It memorialized its way of doing things and incorporated them into a living set of 'Founding Principles' and a 'Statement of Purpose' composed in 1997 and highlighted even today in the company's annual report.

The inclusive process Lonnie used to create the company's culture established Lonnie's credibility as Intuitive's leader. Perhaps the best indicator of hyper-performance in an organization is cultural alignment. Lonnie recognized the importance of starting out with a well-defined culture, a common purpose and getting everyone in alignment around that purpose. He said, "During my career, I had the opportunity to observe many leadership styles and company cultures. I saw Intuitive as an opportunity to try and incorporate the best of what I had learned."

In addition to his leadership skills, Lonnie possessed business discipline. He challenged management to think about and help define Intuitive's business model early as it transitioned to an operating company. Russell Hirsch said, "Lonnie was a business visionary. He challenged the board and management to help refine Fred's vision from a brilliant technical idea to a legitimate business opportunity."

In line with that thinking, Lonnie tested the company's assumptions relative to its early clinical focus. Initially, the company set its sights on the formidable challenge of using its robots to perform minimally invasive coronary artery bypass surgery. What made this such a challenge was the need to design a machine which could work around a heart that was beating and moving.

Lonnie said, "We had hired a consulting firm to help us track a beating heart so we could design the robot to move with the heart while performing beating heart surgery. I was in the process of raising a second round of financing to keep us from running out of money. We were nowhere near a viable design of our basic surgical robot, and we were about to complicate the task by adding the ability of the entire machine to track a beating heart. I had to shut it down." Lonnie felt the added complexity of pursuing this type of surgery would dramatically increase their costs and time to develop a commercial product. He believed the risks of such a challenging project far outweighed the benefits. Intuitive needed to complete the design of the basic surgical robot first.

In addition to recognizing the company was going after the wrong procedure, Lonnie knew he couldn't build a high growth company selling costly capital equipment alone. He needed to build a surgical procedure-based business focused on usage and adoption. Dave Rosa said, "Lonnie focused on metrics measuring usage of the platform and usage by procedure." Towards the end of 2001, Lonnie noted one clinical procedure exhibited a positive usage trend. "Prostatectomies showed consistent growth." Lonnie plotted usage on an adoption curve. "I realized that robotic surgery adoption would occur procedure by procedure and that we had traction in urology."

The robotic prostatectomy was a potentially large market for Intuitive. The company made investments to show clinical efficacy, to train surgeons, and to educate patients and doctors. Adoption was dramatic. One New York urologist said, "After purchasing our first robot, urology booked it for days at a time. Soon, we could only book it for a few hours at a time. We needed a second robot to meet patient demand."

Intuitive gained confidence that sustained company growth would be driven by specific surgical procedure adoption, such as a prostatectomy, across other surgical specialties. With adoption, sales cycles shortened and revenue increased as hospitals tested and bought the DaVinci robot. Hospitals competed with one another. An early buyer marketed the robot in the community to generate consumer awareness. Patients then began asking about robotic surgery. If one institution had a robot, its competitors felt pressure to buy a robot too.

With the strategy of usage and adoption, the company also developed a line of so called 'resposable' surgical instruments, i.e. devices that were neither totally disposable nor totally reusable. Each surgical instrument was designed to have a finite effective life. This required hospitals to replace the instruments repeatedly for the life of the robot. This became Intuitive's razor and blade model, a key component of the company's highly profitable business model.

To succeed, Lonnie had to confront many operational challenges particular to young capital equipment companies. He challenged lean teams to manage lengthy timelines and complex design processes. He pushed product development to design early generation products with the minimum features necessary, and no more. One time, the company was on its third iteration of a design. Everyone had ideas on more improvements. Lonnie asked the youngest engineer in the room, Dave Rosa, for his input. Dave said, "I think it's good enough and we have more important things to do." Fred Moll distinctly remembers that meeting. "You have to see through stages of new product development and ask what's most important. Saying that is one thing. Lonnie made it happen." Lonnie recounted, "We did as Dave suggested and moved on."

Dave Rosa reflected, "Lonnie forced teams to problem solve not by throwing resources at them but with small, nimble teams, and holding them accountable." This was by design. Lonnie deliberately set out Intuitive's eight founding principles to guide the operation of the company. One of these principles, *Small teams win,* states, "We believe in small, agile teams of outstanding staff that deliver results." A second principle is *Believe the beliefs, Deliver the results.* Dave said, "Accountability was a really, really big deal at Intuitive. Lonnie hired great people, held them to a high standard and made changes when needed."

Another example of Lonnie's focus on accountability comes from a story he recounted of an engineer leading a system redesign. Lonnie said, "He was skilled at creating Gantt charts but a weak technical leader. I told his manager the engineer needed to be replaced. The manager asked why and I said the engineer tried to lead the team over the hill twice. I doubted they would follow him a third time. Who should replace him? I suggested Gary Guthart as our best leader." Fast forward over a number of years and Gary is now CEO of Intuitive. Lonnie had a great eye for talent.

Lonnie instituted processes to ensure innovation and product development would stay ahead of the market. He introduced future generations of products to maintain their market leading position. This drive to innovate was also reflected in Intuitive's founding principle, "Innovation is essential to our success."

Lonnie brought discipline to the organization's Intellectual Property (IP) strategy and constantly enhanced its IP portfolio. At Intuitive, plaques of issued patents cover an entire wall. IP strategy was a critical component of the company culture. Fred Moll said, "A sophisticated and aggressive IP policy was in our DNA."

Lonnie taught discipline and focus around margins and manufacturability, which young engineers integrated into their thinking. As to margins, Intuitive has been able to successfully achieve 75% gross profit margins at scale. Their robot is a million dollar piece of capital equipment with 3,000 parts. The operating challenge of achieving positive margins was real. Leadership met those challenges and helped determine the company's destiny.

Lonnie also had a soft side. Dave Rosa said, "Lonnie constantly walked the building, speaking with team members, asking about families, often by name. He was a teacher and a prolific reader and used several books to inform his business acumen." A favorite book was *Barbarians to Bureaucrats: Corporate Life Cycle Strategies*. According to Dave, "It really informed one of Lonnie's core beliefs. Larger companies drift towards bloat with more money being spent on non-core activities. Lonnie pledged it would not happen here at Intuitive."

Lonnie has been described as humble, honest, empowering, a great teacher, and a consummate professional. He set high standards. He held people accountable. He established a high performance culture and an operating framework designed to produce sustainable and consistent results. Having worked with many CEOs while at Mayfield Fund, Russell Hirsch recognized Lonnie as one of very few executives who could lead Intuitive's complex technology and business challenge to success. He said, "Lonnie lived in the details of every functional silo. In the end, he could bring the disparate parts together to maximize value." Dave Rosa added, "Lonnie struck a perfect balance between caring and humble, and relentless accountability."

As investors, our goal is to maximize returns in a reasonable period of time while assuming the lowest possible risk. Experience teaches investors that a great leader and team can maximize the probability of solid returns and therefore ranks at or close to the top of the list of factors we consider before writing a check. Research confirms startup success often depends on leadership and teams' knowledge, passion and aligned objectives. Capable leadership of this type is what drove the success at Intuitive.

Intuitive Surgical had a successful IPO in 2000. Today, the company dominates the medical robotics market. Leadership's vision has remained clear, strong and enduring. They currently enjoy annual revenues of $4 billion and an astounding $67 billion market cap. To date they have sold more than 6,000 robotic platforms used to perform eight million procedures globally. Lonnie Smith recently retired as company Chairman. Fred Moll left to found several other robotics companies. Fred predicted "Robotics would become the future of surgery." It has. Intuitive is a model for entrepreneurs and investors, alike. It is perhaps one of the strongest demonstrations of the principle that success is about great leadership and a great team.

Chapter Nine

The Importance of Investing Human Capital

When you combine great leadership with a strong board of directors, the likelihood of a successful outcome for a business increases by an order of magnitude. Legally, directors are required to provide governance and oversight. However, truly engaged and knowledgeable directors can add significant additional value by providing strategic input and advice. As members of the board, they occupy leadership positions. While that leadership is not always explicit, it can manifest itself in many ways. A truly engaged board adds value and demonstrates leadership in many ways. Examples include recruiting members of the senior management team, assisting with raising new financing to grow the business, helping with introductions to key customers, evaluating and developing the CEO and management team, and influencing a successful financial exit for investors.

Christopher, Joe and I have had the good fortune of working on boards with great investors who have enthusiastically given a company much more than just cash. These investors are true value-add directors. They have positively and significantly impacted shareholder value. That impact, of course, can range from driving higher exit values to navigating crises which threaten the company's very existence.

Avedro is an example where investors, serving as directors and leaders, both positively impacted the company's likelihood of survival and helped maximize enterprise value. These investors were deeply engaged alongside management in company building, team building and crisis management.

The story of Avedro began with David Muller. Early in his career, David founded and led Summit Technologies which was a pioneer in the use of laser technology to correct vision by altering the shape of the cornea. This simple, outpatient procedure, known as Lasik, has been successfully performed millions of times by ophthalmologists throughout the world.

In 2002, several years after leaving Summit, David founded Avedro to continue his early work with corneal disease. He licensed technology from Dartmouth College, and, because of his Summit reputation, was able to raise financing from several venture funds. He set out to develop novel treatments for corneal disease.

The company's first product was a drug plus device therapy to treat keratoconus. Keratoconus is an under-diagnosed disease, often beginning in childhood, for which there is no readily available and effective therapy. It is a disease where the cornea weakens and thins over time. This causes the development of a cone-like bulge and optical irregularity of the cornea. The disease can result in significant vision loss and can lead to a corneal transplant.

David believed the keratoconus market opportunity was relatively modest. But, the disease was one without an effective treatment. Avedro's strategy was to demonstrate safety and efficacy of their existing novel drug-device combination to the Food and Drug Administration (FDA), which might pave the way for future clinical indications, i.e. medical challenges requiring treatment. For their first indication, keratoconus, their expectation was they would obtain FDA clearance and then begin a market introduction of the product. This would allow Avedro to generate early revenue, and create awareness of the potential of their technology to treat other indications.

The company believed their strategy would simplify the regulatory path for future applications of their technology. Their goal was to obtain subsequent clearance of other higher volume and potentially more lucrative clinical applications after securing their initial approval. For example, the company believed its technology could successfully treat myopia (i.e. nearsightedness) which affects many millions of people.

But first, the company had to develop a working treatment for keratoconus. This turned into a long expensive process that required seven years of development before performing the treatment on its first clinical patient in 2009.

Avedro's regulatory strategy made sense to management and its venture investor-heavy board. But, somehow the regulators at the FDA viewed this drug-device combination as much more novel and complex than the company expected. The FDA turned down Avedro's first application for market clearance.

The agency advised the company that clearance would be contingent on positive results generated from significantly more clinical testing than the company had completed at the time of their initial FDA application. After several years accumulating more data, Avedro filed their second application for clearance in March 2015. Despite a panel of experts recommending approval, the FDA turned them down a second time. This was devastating news for the company. And, it wasn't anticipated by the Avedro management team or the board. It meant a much longer approval timeline, and it meant this thirteen year old company would require substantial additional capital.

The company's existing investor base was surprised by this setback, frustrated with management's lack of progress, and unwilling to continue backing the company. By the time of the second FDA rejection, Avedro's journey had already been a long, tortuous process. To put it into personal perspective, one of the earliest investors, Phil Ferneau at Borealis Ventures said, "When we first invested in 2003, my oldest daughter was in first grade. By the time the company exited, she was graduating from Dartmouth."

Most of Avedro's investors were not native to the medical device world. During their collective history with Avedro they had very little input on the strategy and direction of the company. These investors had the best of intentions, but management did not often look to them for advice and counsel. Relegated to the sidelines, the investors had to content themselves with the hope that in time, something positive would come of their investment.

Despite the disappointing second FDA rejection and investor frustration, David Muller, Avedro's CEO, was not willing to give up. He still believed in Avedro's potential. And so, he began beating the bushes looking for new investors. David quickly identified several prospects.

One investor stood out for a number of reasons. Dr. Gil Kliman is a general partner at Interwest Partners. Interwest is a prominent and successful venture capital investor in the life sciences, and specifically ophthalmology. Moreover, Dr. Kliman is a board certified ophthalmologist who trained at the University of Pennsylvania School of Medicine and completed his training in ophthalmology at The Wills Eye Institute and The Massachusetts Eye and Ear Infirmary. Some years later, he completed his MBA at Stanford's Graduate School of Business and began a second career in venture capital.

Gil's industry resume speaks for itself. He had several high profile investment successes in ophthalmology. He was a regular attendee at all the major specialty meetings, and he had a superb network in the industry. And to top it off, Gil co-founded the Ophthalmology Innovation Summit (OIS), which showcased the latest and greatest innovations in the ophthalmic device industry at its sold out annual conferences.

Prior to David reaching out, Gil had been following Avedro's progress. He understood its potential. On paper, Interwest was the definition of a perfect Avedro investor. Arguably, there could not have been a higher potential value-add investor for the company. Gil understood what David was trying to do and believed in the company's technology. He had followed the company's long and tortured history and was curious enough to take a meeting with David and his team.

Gil came away from his meeting at Avedro even more intrigued. He asked Reza Zadno, an entrepreneur-in-residence at Interwest, to take a much closer look at Avedro. Reza was a star in his own right. He was a Ph.D. trained engineer, a successful serial entrepreneur, and had led multiple medical device companies to successful exits including a first-of-breed ophthalmic device company. He came away from his due diligence enthused about the company and its prospects.

Reza said of Avedro, "The product worked and it was safe. Given recent market research, I really believed the initial target market for the treatment of keratoconus was much bigger than the company believed." Reza met with Gil to discuss making an investment and in the end, recommended that Gil and Interwest lead a new round of financing in Avedro. Gil agreed.

When asked about his motivation to invest, Gil said, "My passion is to help bring first-of-a-kind ophthalmic innovations to market that can dramatically improve care. Avedro was an ideal opportunity, being a pioneer in developing a breakthrough treatment to treat a potentially blinding eye disease. I was excited by the potential that, with the right resources, corneal cross linking technology for keratoconus could earn FDA approval and become highly successful around the world."

As a value-add investor Gil knew his first task was to enlist co-investors to fill out the round of financing. His initial call was to Jonathan Silverstein at Orbimed, another highly respected and substantial healthcare investor. Gil successfully worked with

Jonathan in the past when they co-invested in Glaukos, an ophthalmic medical device company. There were a lot of similarities between Avedro and Glaukos. Both companies were in the ophthalmic device industry. And, both companies had experienced an extended timeline to get to market along with a number of unanticipated financings.

Jonathan agreed to co-invest with Gil and Interwest. Jonathan emphasized, "I trusted Gil's clinical judgement and I liked the ophthalmic space. Avedro had a clinical solution to a bad disease no one else could offer. I wanted in."

Toward the end of 2015, Interwest and Orbimed made a financing offer to the company. It was aggressive. It was highly dilutive to existing investors, but Avedro needed the money. The investors were high quality and the company had no viable alternatives. Immediately after their investment of financial capital, Gil and Jonathan began to contribute an incalculable amount of valuable human capital.

They began their efforts at the top. After what the company had been through they knew they needed to identify and hire a new CEO. They constructed a specification for the ideal leader. Based on what they believed the company's most immediate needs were, they realized the best potential CEO candidate was hiding in plain sight, Reza Zadno.

Reza had completed the due diligence on behalf of Interwest. He understood the value of the technology. He was an experienced and successful leader who had led multiple companies to successful outcomes. He had the technical background to contribute to the product's continued development.

The offer flattered Reza, but he was not sure he wanted a full time CEO job, especially with a company located on the opposite coast from where he lived. However, after some time to consider the opportunity, he ultimately agreed to join Avedro as a consultant and acting CEO in early 2016. Soon after, he accepted an offer to join as full time CEO in July 2016.

Given his experience with the company, its people and its challenges, Reza knew what he was getting into. This knowledge, combined with his excellent relationship with Gil and Jonathan, allowed him to hit the ground running. The opportunity was exciting for him and he was thrilled to be working with Gil and Jonathan once again.

Reza said, "Not all money is the same. I had worked with Gil. And he knows the target customer very well, literally. He is a board member who attends all ophthalmic conferences, symposiums and advisory meetings and feeds market knowledge and perspective back into the company. Yet he does all that without micromanaging or interfering in the day-to-day company business. Jonathan, meanwhile, is a one-of-a-kind investor. He is your business conscience. You better listen to him if you want to succeed."

The company board was now composed of Gil, Jonathan, one industry independent director, and two of the early investors. Reza's first order of business was to challenge Avedro's assumptions relative to its go-to-market strategy. During extensive discussions with his board, Reza recommended a shift to the company's thinking. His extensive market research showed the keratoconus market size was likely much larger than early estimates by the company's initial management team.

With the board's guidance and approval, Avedro repositioned itself in anticipation of building a sustainable business around the keratoconus indication. Reza explains, "The disconnect between early estimates and our more optimistic estimates was based on clinician underdiagnosis. Because there were no effective therapies for keratoconus, there weren't any effective diagnostic tools available." Gil, a highly networked and trained ophthalmologist, consulted with colleagues and friends to confirm Reza's thinking.

Avedro began to make progress, received its FDA approval later in 2016 and experienced accelerated revenue growth. In anticipation of future financings and even a possible public offering, Reza, Gil and Jonathan knew they needed to restructure and strengthen the company's board. As part of this process, Gil and Jonathan made sure the board was less venture investor centric.

First, the company recruited a retired Fortune 500 public company CFO to join the company in anticipation of a public offering. The company was fortunate to get someone of his caliber. Next, at Gil and Jonathan's urging, they recruited Tom Burns. Tom was the CEO of Glaukos, a successful public company in the ophthalmic device industry and a portfolio company of Interwest and Orbimed. Tom was someone with experience launching a disruptive new device in the ophthalmology market. Tom was a timely and impactful addition to the board.

Finally, they recruited Bob Palmisano, at the time the CEO of a large, public orthopedic device company. Bob had also served as the CEO of Intralase, a very successful ophthalmic capital equipment company. Bob was a well known and universally respected senior operating executive. With the addition of these strong leaders, the board was more execution oriented, especially in the area of commercial operations in ophthalmology.

Working closely with Reza, the board evaluated Avedro's management team, and where appropriate, made changes. Recruiting and hiring top management talent is a big responsibility for a board. This was a case where the personal networks of the board really mattered. Gil and Jonathan were able to put together a long list of prospects for multiple positions based on the needs identified by management as the company's near term priorities.

One immediate position to fill was the CFO. At the time, this position was vacant. With the company's needs for future financings and a possible IPO, a highly experienced senior executive would be required. Again, in the course of a board meeting, the directors nailed down a job specification and discussed potential candidates. In a matter of months, an experienced senior executive from the medical device industry, with public company and M&A experience, filled the position. Other key management team hires included the chief commercial officer and the executive who would develop broad-based insurance coverage for Avedro's product.

By working closely with its experienced board of directors, Avedro's new management team made tremendous, deliberate progress in approximately three years. By 2018, the company had rapidly-growing revenue for a product that treated keratoconus, a disease with no previous cure. The market for their product was growing. And, the company had intellectual property that would keep competitors at bay for the foreseeable future. It was finally time to think about a public offering for Avedro's stock.

Gil, Jonathan and their colleagues on the Avedro board were well known in the investment banking community. The board's reputation helped with the perception of Avedro as a hot company. Several tier-one bankers, knowing the quality of both Gil's and Jonathan's industry connections, wanted to be part of taking Avedro public. In the end, JP Morgan and BofA Merrill Lynch led the IPO. On February 14, 2019, Avedro completed a public offering, which was not only successful, but also exceeded everyone's expectations. It looked like a fitting end for the investors and employees who had given so much over the years to bring this important product to market.

But the story was not over. During the Summer of 2019, an acquisition offer surprised Avedro. The offer was an all stock offer, and it was from Glaukos. Tom Burns, the CEO of Glaukos and an Avedro board member, disclosed to the board his company's desire to make an offer. Due to his conflicted interests, Tom had to resign from the Avedro board. Avedro's board and management team were taken aback. They could only speculate as to what provoked this sudden and very good offer. It soon became clear. In making the case for the deal to the Avedro team, Tom revealed that Glaukos viewed Avedro as a key component of its future growth strategy.

After years of setbacks and frustrations, Avedro finally succeeded. The merger was completed in November 2019. Although Gil stepped down from both boards in the course of the transaction, he later rejoined the Glaukos board of directors. Reza went on, yet again, to assume the CEO role of a venture-backed medical device company in the growing medical robotics market.

Avedro is a powerful example of great investors exercising leadership by bringing so much more to the table than just money. They helped Avedro's senior leadership to better meet the company's needs. Gil Kliman and Jonathan Silverstein introduced Glaukos' CEO to Avedro and recruited him to their board. They knew Glaukos well as early investors, and recognized potential synergies between Avedro and Glaukos. The potential they recognized and the team connections they made were key to creating the successful outcome the company experienced.

We have seen it time and time again. Investors who become board members can be great partners to a CEO and the management team. Their combined resources can help management and the company achieve their lofty goals. A great entrepreneur will recognize the contributions a great board can make, and be sure to enlist board members as partners in the long road to success.

Theme Three

Does Smart Money Invest in Bits or Atoms?

"When you are investing other people's money, you need to be mindful of where the timelines are shortest and the path easiest. And that has been bits for the totality of my investing career."

Fred Wilson

Chapter Ten

David vs. Goliath

Time and money have an interesting way of changing the landscape we live in. This is especially true in the world of computers. In 1965, while he was CEO of Intel, Gordon Moore published a paper which predicted the number of transistors on a computer chip would double every two years for at least the next ten years.

Moore's prediction held true and continued, albeit at a slightly reduced pace, till around 2012. His conclusions became known as Moore's Law, and provided a roadmap for the rapid growth in computing power. With more transistors on each chip, the speed of computing increased commensurately. As difficult as it might be to believe, the main processor in an Apple iPhone from 2020 is millions of times faster than the CPU processor in an IBM PC from the early 1990s.

Starting with my early teen years, I was a first hand witness to this rapid evolution in technology. My connection with computers began at the middle school I attended in Baltimore, Maryland. The school had a Hewlett Packard computer we could program using punch cards. During math class, I would write simple programs in BASIC, and then place my stack of cards into a basket in the back of the classroom. The next day the math teacher would hand me a printout containing a listing of my program along with the resulting output. If I had a single error in my program, I would have to fix it, resubmit my punch cards, and wait an entire day before I received a new printout. I was fascinated with computers and loved writing programs, but the inability to have immediate results frustrated me.

By the time I was in high school, personal computers hit the scene. Now, I was able to write programs and see immediate results. I was a natural at writing software. I spent as much time as I could in the computer lab whenever I had a break in my daily schedule.

In 1979, immediately prior to my freshman year in college, Brown University launched its Computer Science (CS) Department. Brown became one of the first universities to put together a comprehensive course of study in CS. Under the leadership of Andy van Dam, Brown became a pioneer in the field of computer graphics. When it came time for me to choose a major, CS was a given, and Andy influenced me to focus my research in computer graphics.

While studying at Brown, I spent two years working for Jim Head at the Planetary Geology department. As part of his research on planetary systems, Jim worked on a number of NASA interplanetary missions. My project for Jim focused on developing 2D and 3D models of the planet Venus. Working in a dark room filled with computer equipment, I would spend days at a time cranking out code.

I had access to data collected from NASA's Pioneer Venus mission in addition to data collected from the Arecibo Observatory in Puerto Rico. Combining these datasets, I created the first three dimensional flybys of the planetary surface of Venus. Seeing Jim's eyes light up the first time he saw one of these flybys was one of the highlights of my time in college.

In the early 1980s, real time 3D graphics required powerful computer systems costing hundreds of thousands of dollars. Only large corporations and research universities could afford such equipment. My research at Brown was made possible because I was working at a university with the resources to acquire and maintain expensive computer graphics hardware. A world with inexpensive, widely adopted 3D graphics was still over a decade away.

My early post college career allowed me to continue creating powerful computer graphics software for the avionics and pharmaceutical industries. I ventured into the world of computer hardware a few years after meeting Bill Poduska in 1986. At the time, I was working for a drug discovery software company called Polygen. Bill was one of the most prolific tech entrepreneurs in the country. With a PhD in Electrical Engineering from MIT, Bill is a brilliant engineer and a great business leader. And, he is one of the most gregarious, friendly individuals you will ever meet.

In the 1970s and 1980s, Bill co-founded two major computer companies, Prime Computer and Apollo Computer. Both companies became very successful, publicly traded companies. When I first met Bill, he was introducing his third startup, Stellar Computer. For this startup, Bill assembled a world class team of software and hardware engineers along with experts in manufacturing, finance, sales and marketing.

Stellar's mission was to build the world's first graphics supercomputer at an affordable price. This was a goal near and dear to my interests. Their initial product, called the GS1000, helped scientists and engineers solve challenging problems in areas as varied as weather modeling, drug discovery, nuclear simulation and engineering analysis. These are tasks that were beyond the scope of all but the most expensive computers at the time.

Bill's enthusiasm for Stellar was infectious. After hearing him speak at a local tech event, I wanted to learn more about the company. Based on what I heard from Bill, I felt the GS1000 would be a perfect fit for the software I was developing. And so

Polygen became one of Stellar's first customers. I was one of the early engineers given the opportunity to utilize this new generation of graphics supercomputers.

A year or so after Polygen bought its first GS1000, Stellar reached out to me and asked if I might join their company to help further the development of their computers. After interviewing with Bill's management team, I was all in. How could I turn down their offer to change the world of high performance computing?

I joined Stellar in 1989 at a time when the company had two main competitors, Silicon Graphics (SGI) and Ardent Computer. Stellar, SGI and Ardent sold workstations to scientists and engineers with prices ranging from $50,000 to well over $100,000. Our target customer had funding for such a large expense because the problems they were trying to solve had urgent, real world implications. Designing a new airplane engine or modeling a nuclear simulation must be done right or the consequences are severe. Companies like Boeing and Airbus, and national labs, including Lawrence Livermore and Argonne, needed our sophisticated computers to do their job.

Stellar, SGI and Ardent had brisk businesses because the personal computers of the time from companies such as IBM, Dell and Compaq didn't have enough horsepower to take on these complex and demanding computing challenges. All of the PC companies used CPU chips designed by Intel and AMD to power their machines. In the late 1980s and early 1990s, those chips were quite limited in the tasks they could handle. So SGI, Ardent and Stellar all chose to build custom chips and develop proprietary software to deliver the performance their customers needed.

When Bill Poduska launched Stellar, he knew the company would face many serious challenges. The technical hurdles to move his vision from paper to reality were daunting. However, Bill's successful track record at his earlier startups, Prime and

Apollo, allowed him to recruit some of the best engineers in the world and to raise financing from top tier VCs. In short order, Bill pulled together the human and financial resources he needed to get an amazing initial product to market.

Even with an incredible amount of talent and money at their disposal, Stellar faced an uphill battle typical of situations when small hardware startups compete against large, highly-profitable companies. In the beginning, Stellar saw their main competition come from similarly sized companies in Ardent and SGI. In time, the competition came from industry giants such as Intel and IBM.

As it would turn out, a lack of perspective about Moore's Law and a few more years of exponential growth in transistors on a computer chip led to one of the biggest mistakes made by Stellar and its competitors. They completely misunderstood the impact of massive financial resources on their market. In 1985 (the year Stellar was founded) Intel released its Intel386 chip. This chip could perform up to 4 Million Instructions Per Second (MIPS). That was more than enough speed to efficiently perform basic productivity tasks such as spreadsheets and word processing. But if you wanted to model a complex weather system, these chips would take forever, if they could do it at all. Stellar's first CPU performed at 25 MIPS alongside a co-processor that did an additional 40 Million Floating Operations Per Second (MFLOPS). For most scientific applications, the GS1000 was 10 to 100 times faster than a PC.

Just four years later, Intel had leveraged its massive R&D organization to introduce a new chip called the 486. Weighing in at roughly the same size, it ran five times as fast at 20 MIPS. At that time Stellar introduced the GS2000 which could still perform at a rate of 25 MIPS but with double the rated MFLOPS at 80. Because of the massive resources Intel could throw at R&D, the speed differential between Stellar and the ubiquitous PC was rapidly shrinking.

Designing custom hardware is expensive and time consuming. This is especially true with extremely complex, specialized and difficult to manufacture hardware like computer CPUs. Massive resources allow tremendous leaps forward. For a small startup like Stellar, it was hard to keep pace with well-funded companies like Intel. In 1989, Intel had revenues of $3.1 billion and spent $365 million in R&D. Stellar's revenues were less than one percent of Intel's. And, their R&D budget was less than five percent of Intel's.

Although it was not clear at the time, in hindsight, the end result was inevitable. It was only a matter of time before the massive resources thrown at inexpensive, commodity PCs with Intel CPUs would make them competitive with the speed of the specialty high performance graphics supercomputers from SGI, Ardent and Stellar. When Stellar launched in 1985, Bill and his engineering team were confident they could maintain a significant performance gap over the likes of Intel. But in the end, Moore's Law and a huge R&D budget allowed Intel to close the performance gap and put companies like Stellar and Ardent out of business. This was a case where David could not defeat Goliath.

Even after merging their two companies, Stellar and Ardent were unable to compete. The combined company, called Stardent, shut down towards the end of 1991 having burned through more than $200 million in venture capital. SGI was able to hold on longer, but it too ran into serious headwinds. Ultimately, SGI went bankrupt in 2009 and had a fire sale for their remaining assets.

At its core, Stellar was a computer hardware company with all of the financial and logistical challenges faced when producing a physical product. Hardware companies sell physical *atoms* as contrasted with the intangible *bits* of software products.

Hardware companies, like Stellar, have different economics and cost structures than software companies. They have longer, more complex design processes. They are less nimble and adaptable in terms of redesign if they are caught out of step. They have long supply chains. They consume capital for inventory. And their sales cycles are typically longer if pilots and capital budgeting processes are involved.

As a result, hardware companies have thinner margins which leave less room for error in their business plans. But, if you can overcome these hurdles to success, you will have built a huge moat that will keep the competition at bay. And, your investors will be very happy.

In our theme on "bits vs. atoms", we will dive into the stories of two more hardware companies, Powerhouse Dynamics and Mobius Imaging. Both companies had an accomplished CEO with many years of hardware experience. They knew the challenges they would face before they took a leap of faith and launched their businesses. Although both companies ended up being acquired, the financial outcome for their investors was vastly different.

My experience at Stellar was an incredible learning opportunity for me. It was my first time working for a hardware company. I had a front row seat to witness how difficult it is to be successful building physical products. I learned my lesson well, and quickly returned to the software industry to continue my career selling bits.

Chapter Eleven

Hardware is Hard

As he sits looking out the window of his brick and beam office in an old converted mill building outside of Boston, it's hard for serial entrepreneur-turned-intrapreneur Martin Flusberg not to shake his head. His company Powerhouse Dynamics has taken him on a wild ride. The company was recently acquired by a multi-billion-dollar conglomerate called Middleby. The name is new, but his job is basically the same. He's in a good place in terms of his role, his product, his employees, and his customers, but, it's not exactly the outcome he wanted or expected. Despite his prior experience, he could never have predicted the path he'd go down or the situation in which he'd land.

Martin is living proof of the adage "hardware is hard." In fact, hardware startups are so tricky to manage that they can surprise even an experienced professional with knowledge of what to expect. These startups have a reputation with most investors for presenting more complexity and higher risk. Yet hardware startups can be very rewarding when they work. As a result, optimistic investors cannot help but chase them. This is a story about one that lived up to the bad reputation.

The challenges at Powerhouse Dynamics cannot be chalked up to a lack of education or experience on Martin's part. Martin received an electrical engineering degree from The City University of New York, after which he earned an MS in civil engineering from MIT and ultimately joined the MIT faculty. In the end, his education and career gave him plenty of experience in both hardware and software.

Martin left MIT to join a faculty start-up initially focused on structural engineering software which morphed into a software and services company focused on transportation and construction management. It was named Multisystems. Despite being hired for a technical engineering role, a very early assignment led to the discovery that he could write sales proposals. Martin was immediately swept into the sales function. Recalling those days, he said, "I joke about how in the land of the blind, the one-eyed man is king. I was asked to write a proposal the first week, and we won. And that was the end of my technical career. A number of years later I became the CEO, not something I was expecting. But I discovered I loved it."

After a successful fourteen year run at Multisystems, Martin left for a director role at defense contractor TASC, where he was hired to run a commercial software division serving the utility and real estate industries. This provided him with a foundation in both facilities management and electrical utilities. About six years into that role the siren song of the dot.com revolution came calling. He left to co-found and serve as President of Nexus Energy Software, a provider of software solutions to the utility industry. The company was ultimately sold to ESCO, a public company that had spun out of Emerson. Nexus later merged with two sister companies. That combination morphed into a quarter-billion dollar global provider of smart grid and energy efficiency solutions known as Aclara Technologies. Navigating through various roles at these companies provided Martin with a new set of skills experiences in developing and supporting hardware products.

When he felt it was time to leave Aclara, Martin knew he wanted to continue in the startup space. "I was a CEO at a very early stage in my career and I seemed to have a high tolerance for the challenges – and pain. I wouldn't do this over and over if

I weren't energized by solving the problems. The highs are so much higher because there are so many lows. I thrive on that. I have the classic mindset of an entrepreneur. I like to build something from scratch, see where it goes and steer it toward some kind of success."

Once free from his CEO position at Aclara, Martin began investing in startups as an angel investor. Not long after, an angel partner approached him with an interesting company called Powerhouse Dynamics. It had novel technology to monitor circuit level electricity usage. The company originally developed the technology to allow sharing a single solar energy array among two or more homes and allocate costs appropriately. The founders thought they could build a business providing residential energy management systems.

When he first heard about it, Martin was skeptical, and his initial reaction was, "Don't even think about it. There's no market for that." But his colleague convinced him to take a look. Martin explained, "They had developed a cost-effective way to monitor circuit level energy use to save on energy costs. After thinking about it, I felt there was a real opportunity serving smaller commercial facilities. They're not served by the traditional energy management systems. Nor are they served by the utilities, who focus on large commercial and industrial customers and the residential market. These under-served commercial facilities, such as restaurant and specialty retail chains, represent a huge market." Convinced an interesting opportunity lurked, Martin jumped in. He knew hardware posed challenges, but he felt he was prepared for them.

As noted in the Stellar Computer introduction to this theme, hardware companies sell physical atoms as contrasted with intangible bits of software products. This means hardware companies have different economics and cost structures than software companies. The design process is more lengthy, redesigns are harder, supply chains are more complex, inventory costs money and the sales cycle can be longer. As a result, hardware companies have narrower margins which leave less room for error in their business plans.

Investors can be very skittish around hardware companies, and that fear makes these types of businesses harder to finance. Martin said, "A large number of traditional investors wouldn't even look at a company selling hardware. I think that's a mistake. Hardware is not intrinsically bad. When artfully integrated with software, it can make for an incredible business with long term staying power. Look at the iPhone. When it was launched it was basically hardware – but it included much more sophisticated software than previous mobile phones. And that turned into a pretty good business. Yet, the fear of hardware persists among many venture investors."

Unlike naïve hardware founders, Martin understood where the trouble spots lurked. He was prepared to make a go of it. With this startup, he figured, it could be different. Martin put up some seed money. He raised an additional chunk from his angel colleagues and re-launched the company.

The challenge he faced day one was the need to completely re-design the product. The original designers created it with the needs of residential customers in mind. The needs of commercial facilities were more complex. This design issue ran right through the very core of the product. The founders of the company had embedded their somewhat limited communications module directly into their monitoring system product. This design was a dead end for commercial customers. To serve the needs of this new user base they were going to need a more powerful communications module that could talk to many different kinds of devices and support diverse protocols.

This required a complete redesign. With hardware re-engineering, once you start to make changes, they flow through everything right down to the circuit board. The company had to use its early money and a lot of time to reengineer the product before they could even begin to show it to commercial customers.

This was not unusual. Hardware startups typically need to consume more investor capital on faith before they receive any commercial validation or revenue to reassure investors. And the costly cycle can repeat every time the product changes to support new market demands. Powerhouse Dynamics evolved continuously. Of course, it was not just the hardware requirements that were different. Commercial customers with multiple facilities and different motivations than consumers also needed different software.

Based on his extensive experience working with utilities and the smart grid, Martin's early vision for the commercial product was that it needed to focus on the equipment, including the monitoring of equipment health. Energy monitoring was key functionality that could lead to bottom line savings, but was not necessarily the most compelling use case. Over time the product would need to expand to perform additional functions.

"Energy usage is important," Martin said, "and this was the cost saving rationale that got us in the door. But if you're a restaurant and your walk-in freezer goes down, you've got a major problem. If you're a retailer in Dallas in August and your HVAC goes down, you've got a major problem." And monitoring only gets you so far in terms of energy savings. Customers want a "set it and forget it" experience, so the ability to control and monitor equipment, and not just HVAC equipment, is very important.

As the company continued to expand its customer base into food and retail, they were pulled into supporting additional functionality. Martin continued, "Of the many ways of addressing food safety, food quality, and food waste, virtually all of it is related to the equipment. If the freezer is running too warm to prevent spoilage, you've got a problem. And over time, we expanded from monitoring and controls into a full IoT (internet of things) platform. We eventually integrated with ovens, fryers, dishwashers, hot storage cabinets, and ice machines. We needed to know everything going on with that equipment in real time so we could spot the markers of failure before they happened. Our product slowly turned into a comprehensive energy and food safety package. We often referred to it as a way to enable the Smart Connected Enterprise."

Each time the scope of functionality increased, it required a re-engineering of the product. In some cases, the changes were mere software tweaks. But the needs of the customer sometimes exceeded the capabilities of the underlying hardware, requiring the replacement of some components. When one component needs replacing, many knock-on effects flow downstream. Circuit boards are redesigned, parts moved around, and cases are resized. Before you can test anything, you need to design and engineer everything, research, locate and acquire test parts, and hand build a testing prototype. All this takes time and money.

This cycle is complicated by the constant pressure to lower per-part cost. One of the challenges with hardware is that every redesign is a mandate to reduce costs of the system to achieve more profit. With field experience, the priority shifts from basic reliability to finding cheaper parts and simpler designs to reduce cost.

Every redesign introduces new variables and new points of potential failure. For example, at one point during a redesign of the Powerhouse gateway module, they realized they could save a little money per unit by switching to a smaller, less expensive power supply. Martin said, "We went from a five-volt to a three-volt power supply. Turned out that was a huge mistake. Yes, it saved a tiny bit of money, but it simply wasn't powerful enough. It created customer issues with the transmitting range to and from wired sensors. You learn some things as you go when you're trying to be more efficient. It doesn't always work."

Powerhouse Dynamics was not immune to supply chain issues either. As a small company, working with a small volume contract manufacturer, they often did not have the clout to get high demand parts. Recalling the challenges, Martin said, "Volume makes a big difference. At times, demand for electronic parts was so high that, unless you were buying in huge volumes, you couldn't even get some parts. And so we had huge delays in the supply chain which wreaked havoc on production. And then we often ended up paying much higher prices to build our product."

These higher costs hurt margins further and aggravated the already difficult effects of having to raise enough money to finance inventory. Martin said, "Financing inventory always had an impact on our business. At any point in time our inventory was more than half a million dollars, and inventory needs to be paid for in advance, in cash. Our biggest market, restaurants, for whatever reason, do not pay on a timely basis. So, we had to put up cash in advance and then wait for customers to pay us for the product." Unlike software, where subsequent copies of the product are instant and free, physical inventory needs to be manufactured, stockpiled, and paid for in advance. This is the fundamental difference between selling atoms versus bits.

Despite best efforts, not all of the inventory could always be turned back into cash. Describing the situation, Martin said, "We always had a sophisticated sales forecasting model that projected how much we'd need by component. But sometimes the sales don't come in or there's a shift in customer priorities. So, for example, at one point we were left with a lot of energy monitors sitting in inventory."

The selling process itself can also present challenges. After a major portion of his career dealing with utilities, Martin was shocked by how restaurants preferred to purchase. His previous utility customers were very hesitant to make capitalized expenditures to buy hardware. But they would happily pay recurring fees. In contrast, restaurant chains strongly preferred to capitalize the cost of both hardware and software. Martin said, "Restaurant margins are so thin that they are just allergic to recurring fees. They would recoil in horror. 'You want to charge me $20 a month? Are you crazy?' Then after work they go home and watch their Netflix subscription. I had to shake my head. We eventually got around this issue by bundling a prepaid two-year license fee up front as part of the initial cost."

Restaurants were also challenging because of their insistence on unnecessary trial pilots to test the product. Martin recalls being frustrated. "I assumed they would make money-saving decisions quickly and decisively. To my great disappointment, I discovered they take just as long as utilities to commit. They'd insist on these pilots, even when there was absolutely no reason to. Corporate headquarters would do a pilot on behalf of all their franchisees, and they'd tell their franchisees, 'You don't have to pilot this. We have tested it and it works great.' And all the franchisees invariably say, 'Oh, but my store is different' when they're not in the least bit different. Same franchisor, same equipment, same store layout, less than 100 miles away. So, here I was excited at the prospect of working with real business people. You know the old saying, be careful what you wish for."

Over the years Powerhouse managed to adapt to the quirks of the industry verticals they served. The company raised investor money multiple times. They insisted on paid pilots with customers regardless of the push back. They occasionally resorted to purchase order financing to overcome restaurants' slow payment practices. They adapted their product to interconnect and control more and more types of equipment. They structured their license fees to upfront payments rather than ongoing subscriptions. And they got better at forecasting sales.

By the time they were acquired, they managed to build a rapidly growing multi-million dollar business. But it took longer than expected. And they never escaped the atmospheric drag effects of being in hardware. Because of slower than expected growth, small top line revenue numbers, and lack of profitability, the company ended up being acquired for a lower revenue multiple than they had been expecting. It was a successful exit in one sense, but definitely not a major win for the investors.

Powerhouse Dynamics was acquired by a multi-billion-dollar conglomerate with nearly 100 subsidiaries and a very small central management team. It was a strategic acquisition to leverage Powerhouse's IoT platform for many of the sister companies.

Martin continues to run the company with almost full autonomy. He likes the acquiring team very much. He is able to continue developing his product and serving his customers. They are actively integrating the platform with the products of peer business units which are helping to generate business for Powerhouse. But as good as his situation is, neither Martin nor his investors expected it to turn out quite this way.

When he founded the company he was an experienced entrepreneur. He was going to beat the odds associated with hardware startups. But the realities of hardware overpowered best intentions. Design process challenges, manufacturing, inventory, financing, slow sales cycles, slow payment - there was just too much financial drag to reach escape velocity. If his investors were not skittish about hardware going in, most of them probably are a bit more cautious now.

Chapter Twelve

It Takes Thrift and Experience

One of the toughest jobs in the business world is the CEO role in a startup company. It's a rare breed of person who has the complex mix of skills to successfully launch and grow a major company. In their never ending search for potentially great companies, investors focus much of their attention on the character and capabilities of founding CEOs. And, two of the most important skills to look for in a CEO are tenacity and the ability to sell.

Tenacity is defined as the ability to persist even in the face of daunting challenges. Life in a startup is a series of highs and lows just like riding a roller coaster. It takes resilience to handle the extremes a CEO sees almost daily. You can't let the good days go to your head or let the bad days get you down. A CEO's tenacity allows her to continue the battle to succeed when others would give up.

And, it goes without saying, selling skills are crucial for a CEO to build a successful business. It's an absolute necessity for a CEO to lead the charge and convince others to join the march. Whether talking to prospective customers, potential investors or future employees, the CEO must be able to sell.

Having known and worked with Gene Gregerson over the past twenty years, I knew he had those two key skills. In 2008, he approached me to help fund his third startup, a medical device company called Mobius Imaging. Gene had sketched out a rough plan to build from scratch a portable CT scanner that would change the way diagnostic imaging would be used in hospital operating rooms. My first reaction was that this is not going to be easy. As things turned out, to pull off this audacious goal, Gene would ultimately have to fight for survival far too many times. And, he had to use his selling skills to convince much larger companies to support the development of his industry-disrupting CT scanner.

Gene grew up in Salt Lake City, the son of a residential home developer. He said, "My father taught me the value of hard work at an early age. During my high school years, he had me help his home building business by hauling lumber and framing houses."

When asked where his tenacity and competitive spirit came from, Gene points to two important periods in his life. "In high school, I became interested in bodybuilding. I had a great teacher help me set ambitious goals in the sport and achieve them. The first Mr. Olympia, Larry Scott, retired to Salt Lake City and opened a personal training business. I trained with Larry, and ultimately, his support was key in my journey to becoming the Utah High School State Champion for bodybuilding."

The next stage in Gene's life was as a mathematics major, first as an undergraduate at BYU Hawaii, and then as a graduate student at Tufts University in Medford, Massachusetts. "I was surprised with how competitive the math department was at BYU Hawaii," said Gene. "The department was small, but the students were really smart. I thrived there as I loved the people, the location, and the studying. When I arrived at Tufts to get my graduate degree, I realized that I had to take it up another notch. At Tufts I was competing against some of the top math students in the country." It was through lessons learned during these years of bodybuilding and math competition that Gene developed the tenacity and mental strength he would need to be a successful startup CEO.

So where did a young bodybuilding champion, math major from Utah learn how to sell? Extreme mathematical ability is often associated with introversion, and sales undoubtedly requires the skills of an extrovert. Gene's path to developing his sales skills is unusual. Growing up in Utah, Gene was raised as a member of the Church of Jesus Christ of Latter-day Saints. As part of his commitment to the church, Gene served as a missionary in Brazil for two years.

"It was a very eye opening experience for me," said Gene. "I grew up in a community in Utah that was not diverse, whereas Brazil was. It was the first time I witnessed extreme poverty and understood just how some people must struggle in life. I lived and worked in poor, dangerous areas. During my time as a missionary, I learned how to sell. As you can well imagine, it was not easy recruiting new members to my church in a country that is predominantly Catholic. One key lesson I learned during my time in Brazil is I can only sell what I truly believe in."

Gene was introduced to the world of medical imaging while he was a graduate student at Tufts. He studied under Professor Todd Quinto, an expert in the field of tomography. Tomography is a mathematical technique that combines image slices into a three dimensional representation of a physical object. One of tomography's most common uses is with medical imaging devices such as Computed Tomography (CT) scanners.

Gene worked closely with Professor Quinto on unsolved problems posed by Professor Allan Cormack, the Nobel Prize winner for his work on the mathematics of CT. Gene's career never strayed far from the work he began as a graduate student. And today, Gene is one of a small number of people in the world with truly deep expertise in the field of medical imaging.

My first encounter with Gene was in the mid 1990s, a few years after he graduated from Tufts. We were both working for startup companies in Boston. My company, Advanced Visual Systems, built 3D visualization tools used by Gene's company, Visualization Technology Inc. (VTI). VTI was developing an image-guided endoscopic sinus surgery platform. I was impressed with Gene's technical skills, and hoped I would get an opportunity to work with him in the future.

Gene worked at VTI for five years. He said, "I was hired by the CEO, Maurice Ferre. Taking the job at VTI was one of the best career decisions I've made. Maurice was a terrific mentor. I learned so much from him which I still value and use today."

VTI was ultimately acquired by General Electric, and Gene moved from a startup to a Fortune 500 company. Not surprising, it wasn't a good fit for Gene. "While working at GE, I came up with an idea for a new medical imaging device that was a rotating C-Arm," said Gene. "As the device rotated, it would collect multiple image slices. I developed a method to reconstruct 3D models from the slices. I thought it was a great idea, but GE wasn't interested. They weren't willing to fund my product concept."

My second encounter with Gene was in 2003. At the time I had my hands full running an angel group in Boston called Launchpad. Gene approached me looking for funding for his next startup, Breakaway Imaging. Unfortunately, for a variety of not very good reasons, we didn't invest. Breakaway had a quick exit for a medical device startup. Gene was able to launch, build and sell the company in about five years. Investors achieved an excellent return in a short period of time.

Gene's journey with Breakaway Imaging wasn't as easy as I make it sound. Gene recalls vivid memories of an intense, five year effort to launch and build the company. "I woke up one night at 1:00 AM and came up with the idea for Breakaway Imaging. I took out a home equity loan and convinced a colleague to join me at Breakaway. We tried to raise money from VCs but with no luck. Their general feedback to us was, 'If your idea is so great how come GE hasn't done it?' I really resented the whole VC fund raising process."

Just prior to starting Breakaway, Gene was introduced to Dr. Hansen Yuan, a Professor of Orthopaedic and Neurological

Surgery at the State University of New York (SUNY) Upstate Medical University. Having little success raising capital for Breakaway, Gene contacted Dr. Yuan and asked if he would be interested in hearing about his latest idea.

Gene's story of his meeting with Hansen is a classic. "We built a wooden mock-up of our product. We put it in a small U-Haul and drove 300 miles for a meeting with Hansen at SUNY in Syracuse, NY. At the end of our meeting, Hansen slid a check for $500,000 across the table. I love this guy. He has a great demeanor. He knew all the people in our industry. He was a great doctor and a great businessman. And, he helped us raise the financing we needed from his colleagues."

With the necessary capital in hand, Gene began the development of the world's first O-Arm Imaging System. The O-Arm was designed to give orthopedic surgeons detailed 3D views during surgical procedures. It was a medical imaging device with unique capabilities. Dr. Yuan and his colleagues believed the O-Arm would provide the break-through intraoperative visualization they needed to improve patient outcomes.

Breakaway received FDA approval for their product in June 2005. Almost two years later, the company was acquired by Medtronic. Gene and his investors did very well with the payout from Medtronic. But, it had been a long, hard road for Gene over the previous five years. He needed a break to catch his breath and get the rest of his life in order.

Entrepreneurs generally get restless when they sit idle. Gene Gregerson proved to be no exception. After about a year of recovery, Gene was ready to get at it again. He said, "I knew two things. First, there were a lot of limitations with the O-Arm device we created at Breakaway. Second, Medtronic's success with the O-Arm was changing the medical imaging world. I had an idea for a new device that would provide surgeons with even higher quality diagnostic imaging than the O-Arm. And I was ready to launch another company."

"With a rough outline for this new product in mind, I called Dr. Hansen Yuan and asked if he was interested. It didn't take much to convince him to invest in the company, which I had named Mobius, and to join our board of directors. And, once again, Hansen made key introductions to additional investors."

Gene's timing for launching Mobius was both good and bad. In late 2008, the world's economy was plunging into the deepest recession since the 1930s. Raising capital for a startup medical imaging company wasn't going to be easy. But with Dr. Yuan on board as both a co-founder and a financial backer, Gene at least had a start.

When Gene contacted me in early 2009 to ask about an investment from Launchpad, I wasn't going to make the same mistake I made with Breakaway Imaging. Gene presented a compelling case for the concept behind Mobius's mobile CT Scanner. At that time he only had a PowerPoint presentation. However, his track record of success spoke for itself. He's a "jockey" you would be crazy not to back. Despite the pre-prototype stage he was at, we put our trust and money behind Gene.

Building a new CT scanner from scratch is both challenging and expensive under the best of circumstances. What Gene was looking to do was almost an order of magnitude more difficult. His vision for the Airo Scanner was truly audacious. He wanted the device to have three novel features. First, it had to be portable so it could move from one operating room to another. This would save hospitals significant costs with the delivery of imagery. Second, the inner bore, where patients lay, had to be big enough to accommodate large patients and instrumentation during intraoperative imaging. And finally, the Airo needed to integrate with surgical navigation systems to provide real-time updates to the surgeon during an operation.

In order to pull off this challenging trifecta of leading-edge features, Gene had to overcome numerous technical challenges with limited financial and engineering resources. A well-funded company such as GE or Medtronic might take on such a challenge, but they would spend tens if not hundreds of millions of dollars over at least a decade of development to pull off such a difficult product development plan. Gene had neither the luxury of that funding nor the patience for that kind of extended timeline.

Against all odds, Gene was able to build the Airo from scratch in less than four years for less than $10 million of equity financing. This was an extraordinary accomplishment. When asked how he was able to do it, Gene said, "With Mobius, there were five key elements to our success. First, don't invent what you don't need to. Second, more money is not helpful. Third, the best time to start a company is during a bad economy. Fourth, look for sources of non-dilutive financing. And finally, hire a small, talented engineering team."

Let's take a closer look at each of those elements. In order to build the Airo, Gene needed electronic components that didn't exist in 2009. The Airo's design required parts such as x-ray tubes and batteries much smaller than those available at the time. Here's where Gene's amazing selling skills came into play.

"There is a company in almost any niche that does something very well. So, why not get that company to work with you. For example, I approached Varian to develop a custom x-ray tube for us. By selling my vision of Mobius and what Varian would gain by working with us, I was able to convince Varian to take a risk. We didn't have to spend a penny on their development efforts. And, they ended up with a new x-ray tube that's installed in hundreds of scanners around the world," said Gene.

The second success element for Mobius relates to how the company was financed. Gene is a proponent of limiting the amount of capital you raise to launch a business. Gene reflects, "Taking more money is almost always a bad decision. In the middle of difficulty lies opportunity. When you don't have money you stay focused. And, with too much money you have a propensity for waste."

The third element is a bit difficult to control because it relies on when you launch your business. Gene said, "I believe the best time to start a company is during a bad economy. Talent is more widely available. And, companies desperate for new business were willing to do things for Mobius for free that they wouldn't do in a strong economy."

Element four relates to the overall plan for financing a hardware business. Hardware companies are expensive to run. Product development and manufacturing costs are high. And product inventory can eat up a ton of capital.

Gene knew all about these issues from his days at Breakaway. "I didn't want to dilute our investors' ownership in Mobius by taking on a lot of equity financing from VCs. I knew I had a valuable asset that I could use to leverage my financing. Distribution rights for the Airo would be worth a lot when we started shipping the product. I mustered all the sales skills I had and convinced Brainlab, a leading image-guided surgery company, to pay upfront for these distribution rights. Brainlab provided us with significant funding over several years. This helped with our cash flow and reduced our need for additional debt or equity financing," said Gene.

The final element in the ultimate success of Mobius relates to the size of the engineering team. The Airo is a very complex product. A natural inclination would be to hire dozens of engineers to build it. Gene recalls how he took a different approach. "I decided I would take on the role of General Contractor for the product. Just like my father was the GC on the houses he built, I was the GC for the Airo. I built an internal team of ten highly talented engineers, and worked with a small number of outside companies such as Varian to build key components. I kept management overhead low and streamlined communications to get the job done in a timely fashion."

With the successful release of the Airo in 2014, Mobius introduced a groundbreaking technology for image-guided surgery. As is typical in the healthcare industry, bigger companies quickly became interested in Mobius. In the Fall of 2019, Mobius was acquired by Stryker for $500 million. Gene, yet again, delivered a big payday for his investors, his employees and for his family.

Looking back on the ten year journey of Mobius, from original idea until the sale to Stryker, we can extract some important lessons for anyone thinking of launching a company selling sophisticated hardware products. A central element to the company's success ties directly to the selling skills Gene developed as a young man on a mission in Brazil. His ability to convince companies like Varian and Brainlab to back an unknown startup provided him with the financing and technology he so needed. Furthermore, his ability to recruit some of the most talented engineers in Massachusetts ensured the product would be built.

Gene's many years of experience at VTI and Breakaway served as a great learning environment to prepare him for what he needed to do to make Mobius a success. Building a hardware company is hard, but Gene had experience with the key elements that would make his path more straightforward. His journey with Mobius was never easy, but success never is.

Theme Four

What Difference Does Timing Make?

"You don't have to swing hard to hit a home run. If you got
the timing, it'll go."

Yogi Berra

Chapter Thirteen

Better to Be Lucky Than Good

Christopher has been known to quip every now and again, "Sometimes it is better to be lucky than good." Like most humor, this phrase has its foundation in truth. When it comes to different types of luck, good timing can be one of the most powerful kinds of luck you can have. Consider the story of IONA Technologies, where Christopher was an executive from 1997 until 2008. The company had terrifically talented people and very good products, but there can be no disputing that the blessing of good timing played a major role in its success.

IONA was founded by tenured computer science professors, Chris Horn and Sean Baker, at Trinity College in Dublin, Ireland in the early 1990s. The European Union commissioned Chris and Sean to research how to get all the different nations' computer systems to work together in preparation for the tightening of the EU's common market. In doing that research the professors discovered a powerful new software approach being developed by a consortium of enterprise software market participants into a powerful new standard for interoperability between different systems. The professors understood how big a problem computer interoperability was becoming and immediately recognized the commercial potential of this standard.

They decided to found a company to offer the world's first commercial product based on the new standard. Their timing was perfect. It coincided exactly with the growing need for a new breed of software called middleware. Middleware serves as a go-between layer of software integrating other existing software systems. They knew the middleware space was demanding, so they built a fast, powerful and secure product. Their launch timing was perfect, riding the wave of a rapidly growing awareness of the new standard. As a result, the company IONA was born with massive global companies such as Boeing, Lucent, and Motorola amongst its first customers.

Early revenue grew exponentially year over year in the early 1990s as the market for business software grew. Growth was also accelerated by the increasing excitement for the internet and for adding web capabilities into business software. This ultimately led to the frenetic dot.com era associated with the late 1990s.

In a second bout of near perfect timing, in early 1997 IONA chose to go public on the NASDAQ market with investment banking help from Lehman Brothers. The timing of this offering could not have been better given the dot.com boom. The market for technology stocks was not only hot for this kind of IPO, it would continue to rise to dizzying heights for several years to come.

Despite the company being a fairly specialized middleware player, IONA's IPO ended up being among the top five largest software IPOs in history, and the largest since Netscape had gone public and kicked off the dot.com boom. Software was hot, and the company was in the right place at the right time to capitalize on the opportunity in front of them.

Although the dot.com era came to a crashing end in the early 2000s, Christopher recalls the company continuing to thrive commercially by combining a very loyal and stable customer base with a series of well-timed acquisitions and product pivots. "Company leadership paid attention to changes in the market,"

Christopher said, "and were early promoters of emerging trends in software design. They were early to support the business use of web portals. Portals allowed companies to interact with customers directly over the web. The company was similarly early to support the software transition to web standards and service-oriented computing architectures (an early precursor to what we know today as the cloud.) This product nimbleness carried them through the post-dot.com crash years in the early 2000s."

By 2007 fortuitous timing returned to the fore. The company had a large presence and many customers in financial services, so management had early warning of the impending financial meltdown of 2008. As the company was preparing to close its fourth quarter of 2007, two very large customer deals in financial services simply vanished overnight with little warning. Christopher said, "It was clear from talking to these large financial services customers that something serious was afoot in the financial world - more serious than most people grasped."

Christopher was IONA's CFO at that time. Not only did the company pre-announce to Wall Street that it was going to miss the financial targets it had set in its guidance to financial analysts, it also aggressively cut costs fearing the downturn that was to come. Because of the pre-announcement, the company's stock dropped, lowering the company's market capitalization and making the company a more feasible acquisition target.

A competitor in Europe told IONA of its intention to acquire the company. Unfortunately for the acquirer, but perhaps fortunately for IONA in terms of deal timing, the would-be acquirer's bankers leaked details of the acquisition approach to the Irish business press.The resulting articles caused the company's stock to move up on speculation of a deal.

The company was listed on both the NASDAQ market in the US and on the Irish Stock Exchange. The Irish Stock Exchange insisted that the company make what they called a market leveling announcement to make sure all market participants knew the company was the subject of a possible acquisition. NASDAQ's rules required the company to mirror the disclosure in the US. IONA brought its IPO banker Lehman Brothers back in and put out a Securities Exchange Commission ("SEC") 8-K filing in February 2008 announcing that it had hired a banker and was reviewing its strategic alternatives. Fortunately for IONA, that led to terrific interest in the company. By March more than a dozen potential acquirers were evaluating the company.

March was also the month when the 2008 financial meltdown really started to accelerate. Bear Stearns finally succumbed to its overexposure to subprime mortgages and had to sell to JP Morgan for a small fraction of their former high flying value. As the financial world around it continued to grow more shaky, IONA worked on its deal process, narrowing down the pool of bidders and beginning due diligence reviews with the finalists.

As IONA's deal progressed, the economy grew worse. By May, the extent of the mortgage crisis was becoming clear due to the situation at Countrywide Financial. Countrywide, which issued 17% of US mortgages, came under investigation by the FBI for mortgage fraud. They were a serious bankruptcy risk.

IONA's deal continued forward and by June, they were in final negotiations with the ultimate buyer of the company. IONA filed a deal disclosure and investor proxy with the SEC at the end of the month.

July saw the snowballing financial mess gather momentum with a looming liquidity crisis at global insurer AIG. AIG, which had built a huge business insuring other financial companies' bets on mortgage assets, spent the month making a series of announcements about how their liabilities looked likely to exceed their assets. As the month wore on, each shortfall estimate was billions bigger than the previous estimate. At the same time it was becoming clear to the world that storied investment bank Merrill Lynch was at risk of possible collapse due to having too much exposure to bad mortgage related bets.

Perhaps the greatest concern to IONA were the persistent rumors that Lehman Brothers was badly over-exposed to toxic financial instruments and at growing risk of failure. The Lehman Brothers team working with IONA repeatedly denied the rumors and promised there was nothing to worry about. They continually asserted they had heard from Lehman senior management that everything was going to be fine. Since IONA was three quarters of the way through a publicly disclosed acquisition, its leadership team really had little choice but to press ahead with the deal and rely on Lehman as their banker.

As the summer turned to Labor Day and the financial crises gave way to governmental attempts to staunch the bleeding, Christopher headed back to Dublin. After many trips to Dublin over the years, Christopher made one final journey to acquire shareholder approval for the deal at IONA's annual general meeting of shareholders. By then it was clear that Bank of America was going to have to acquire both Countrywide and Merrill Lynch to stave off their collapses. AIG, Fannie Mae (the largest company in the US by total assets), and many other global financial firms were going to need financial bailouts. Lehman Brother's fate was still up in the air, but increasingly dire rumors about them were swirling.

IONA obtained shareholder approval to complete the deal in early September. With approval in hand, Christopher returned to Boston to finalize the closing of the deal. The news was dominated by stories of major financial firms and markets failing, and it was beginning to look like a miracle that the deal might actually be completed. Any doubts about whether the buyer was offering a good price had long evaporated by that point. The alternative option of staying independent and trying to maintain revenue looked less and less attractive in the gathering downturn.

IONA and Lehman Brothers pressed ahead and were ready for the final closing on Friday, September 12th. The day came, the signatures were exchanged, the money was wired, the SEC filings and press announcements were made, and the deal was officially closed. The following morning, Saturday, a mere eighteen hours after the closing, it was announced that Lehman Brothers was bankrupt and was shutting down. Having closed IONA's acquisition on Friday night, Lehman's 161 year history came to an end with a Chapter 11 filing that Monday morning.

Due to its perseverance, and by dint of some tremendously lucky timing, IONA managed to complete a successful sale while the global economy crumbled around them, and their investment bank teetered on the brink. Christopher recalls the feeling of selling the company that September of 2008 as similar to "running from a burning building."

To this day, Christopher marvels at the incredible power of perfect timing. In this fourth theme of the book, we will explore the powerful role of timing in several other startup stories. It is true that good timing alone cannot guarantee the success of a company. Timing falls more into the category of things that are "necessary but not sufficient." But timing undoubtedly plays a major role in startup outcomes. Christopher had many experiences at IONA and learned innumerable lessons, but perhaps the most important lesson he took away is that having good luck on timing might be the best luck of them all.

Chapter Fourteen

Right Product, Wrong Time

When most people think of bad timing in business, they imagine a company that scrambled to jump on an opportunity but showed up with too little, too late. It happens all too often. People can be slow to act on a dawning opportunity and others will beat them to the punch.

A far more heartbreaking example of bad timing occurs when a company shows up way too early for an opportunity and dies waiting for the market to come together. Confer Software was an especially painful example of this dynamic. Their product was built to streamline the delivery of healthcare and was superior to competitors in so many ways. Their vision of how the healthcare market should work was prescient. But they badly misread the state of the market. Customers were just not ready to embrace Confer's solution. The result was a spectacular failure of timing. How could this happen to very smart and talented business people? With the benefit of hindsight, it is not hard to understand the trap they fell into.

Consider the state of the healthcare market in the late 1990s, and, still today in many parts of the system. One day you visit your primary care physician. During the visit, she prescribes certain lab tests, an x-ray, a visit to a specialist, and a follow-up visit with her. This involves four or more paper orders handed to you by the receptionist in order to initiate follow up, make the calls, wait for insurer authorizations, and then schedule the visits.

Wouldn't you prefer if all of these orders could be facilitated automatically by the time you were ready to leave the physician's office? You would walk away from the visit with a care plan, including insurance approvals and all needed appointments made electronically. And, when you showed up for those appointments, you would not need to fill out the same information form each and every time you visit. You know that form... the one asking you to provide your name, address, phone number, insurance, medications, and history of allergies even though you have been working with the same care providers for years and none of your data has changed. Even today, it is hard to believe we still have to fill out these paper forms repeatedly.

In the US, we spend over a trillion dollars per year on healthcare. That enormous sum of money accounts for 17% of our annual GDP. With such a huge percentage of our spending focused on one industry, one would hope we'd operate it as efficiently as possible. Healthcare is still one of our least efficient industries. Our healthcare system wastes many billions of dollars on unnecessary care, redundant tests, excess administrative effort, and medical errors. This is a problem that's been around for a long time. And it turns out to be fiendishly difficult to solve.

Enter Confer Software. Confer's mission was to clean up the healthcare record keeping mess and completely revolutionize the patient experience into a patient-centric, smooth-flowing, continuous care chain. The vision was bold. Without question, Confer had the potential to make a significant impact on a hospital's ability to deliver cost-effective, high quality care. And it was not just theoretical. Confer's hypothesis was successfully demonstrated by its early customers. Despite all of its enormous potential, the broader healthcare market was not ready for what Confer had to offer.

In November 1994, two very smart entrepreneurs, Ken Macrae and Ann Ting, founded Confer Software. Initial financing for the company came from Mayfield Fund, an established and respected Silicon Valley venture capital firm with deep roots in the healthcare industry. The company spent its early days at Mayfield's Sand Hill Road offices, where two of its partners, Bill Unger and Russell Hirsch, were founding members of Confer's board. When asked why Mayfield chose to back Confer, Bill Unger said, "There were many reasons. For one, the Confer software platform automated the delivery of care, no small thing. It facilitated the electronic delivery of orders across the hospital, saving providers and patients lots of time and money. It was the first software platform designed to accelerate the move to more patient-centric healthcare, while sharing important data for analysis and decision making throughout the hospital. All of this resulted in improved quality of care."

At the time of Confer's initial financing, there was significant change afoot in the healthcare market. As is typically the case in healthcare, change was coming slowly but steadily. During the late 1990s and into the early 2000s, healthcare focused on the transition from paper records to the electronic medical record (EMR). The need was obvious. Storing and maintaining patients' paper medical records required a massive amount of costly office space. Besides being an eyesore, it made for inefficient and expensive patient and practice management.

Transitioning to an EMR made sense. It was the common repository and source of patient information. But the transition was a challenge for clinicians and administrators on many levels. Most in the industry thought of the EMR as being just what the world needed. However, it was but one piece of a complex puzzle. For all intents and purposes, the EMR is a digital warehouse for data. Instead of paper, patient information is entered and stored in this digital warehouse. And, the EMR shares data between healthcare professionals throughout the hospital. It sounds fairly straightforward, but its challenges were many.

Installing an EMR in a hospital requires a massive investment of both time and money. Furthermore, it requires years to implement and install, redesigning institutional workflow, followed by a significant investment in training the doctors and nurses who use the system on a daily basis. Because the potential number of variables involved in a typical patient's care are almost limitless, the software must be extremely flexible and feature laden if it is to be relied on to cover every possible scenario. That means it is almost predestined to be very complex for the user. And the facts bear that out. Once it's up and running, there is typically a high level of user dissatisfaction, sometimes up to 40% of users.

Even though the transition to an EMR is a painful, time consuming, and costly process, there is a compelling need for these systems. That need was subsequently reinforced some years later by the US government when system adoption was mandated to the greater market. In order to accelerate the transition, the US government even provided financial incentives to drive adoption.

It was easy for entrepreneurs to view such a market situation as a big potential opportunity. What wasn't easy was for these entrepreneurs to deliver the right product at the right time. Confer launched its initial product during this period of accelerating growth for EMR systems.

When they founded Confer, Ken Macrae and Ann Ting created a compelling vision for the future of the healthcare ecosystem. The "care chain" is the name for this ecosystem. The care chain links all of the components of a healthcare transaction including provider organizations, patients, individual physicians, payors, etc. in a coordinated web of care delivery. Ken wanted to build a product to address all of the components in the care chain. The Confer platform allowed users to take data stored in an EMR, and with this data, they would automate the steps required to deliver a smooth healthcare experience for the patient. That big vision was something which an EMR could not do.

The Confer platform was designed for where the market would someday need to go. Mei Yan Leung, a highly experienced healthcare executive, was Confer's first marketing leader. She said, "The company developed a totally new category of product for healthcare. The product was very disruptive. Confer was trying to help hospitals change the care chain. Our product opened a path to the future."

So, what was the market's reaction to the Confer platform when it was released to the greater market? Philip Bradley joined Confer as Vice President of Sales in 1998. He had a ringside seat to the challenges faced by the company as they introduced a new approach to running the hospital care chain. Phil said, "I came to Confer with my eyes open. Joining the company was an easy decision. The product was a game changer. It could improve the archaic way things are done in the care setting." Ever the optimist, Phil knew Confer's market wasn't ready. And, while time consuming and costly, Confer had to educate the market all by itself on the benefits of its platform. Phil said, "If I believe in the product, and I did, I will stick with it and figure a way to get the job done."

In the early days, Confer's sales team introduced the product to a limited set of target prospects. When reaching out to them, Phil said, "Not one prospect thought the product concept was crazy. While not a ringing endorsement, I viewed their feedback as being a positive indicator. However, there were other more measured comments such as, 'it is so futuristic.' And others looked at the Confer platform as 'competing for dollars against other priorities.'"

Having already spent tens if not hundreds of millions of dollars on licensing, implementing and training for an EMR, hospitals were reluctant to spend money on an additional enterprise system. The biggest, earliest and most established EMR companies used their market dominance to make it very difficult for disruptive new technologies like Confer's to gain market traction. And, it was all the more challenging because Confer's sales reps didn't sell their platform as a traditional EMR. Where the basic EMR category was a need-to-have product, hospitals viewed Confer's more sophisticated platform as a nice-to-have product. They couldn't justify the added cost or required changes to the internal processes used to manage their care chain.

Even with all of those headwinds, the Confer sales team had some success building a paying customer base, which included notable institutions such as UCSF Stanford Health Care, Caremark, and Blue Cross Blue Shield of New Hampshire, among others. That small customer base, however, wasn't adequate to sustain the business and allow for extensive market education.

For the Confer board and management team, limited success selling their product contributed to a period of self assessment. As we know, entrepreneurs love their inventions. They look upon them almost as a child and won't tolerate those around them calling their child ugly. Such was the case at Confer. The product specification came from co-founder, Ken Macrae. Ken's objective was to design a system that would redefine the market and put the competition to shame. But after tremendous effort trying to sell this vision, one conclusion became too obvious to ignore. The Confer platform was a generation or two removed from the state-of-the-market at the time.

There are times when you have to make a major leap forward to be successful. True product visionaries are willing to risk it all to create new, valuable products and services. Steve Jobs did it with the personal computer and again with the smartphone. Jeff Bezos did it with Amazon's comprehensive vision of the potential of eCommerce.

But, sometimes, customers aren't ready to leap too far into the future. They might be afraid of major change to the way they do their job. Or, perhaps they worry the new product won't deliver on its futuristic claims. Or, they don't share the same priorities around what needs to change and when. Whatever the reason, many visionary companies fail because their products are outside their target customer's comfort zone.

While Ken may have achieved his objective of creating a new platform for the healthcare industry, the market had the final say. It was very clear, hospitals were looking for a more basic tool. In Mei Yan Leung's words, "Category creating products, by definition, take a lot more time to gain traction. You need significant funding and patience to educate the market in order to build a community of evangelists, early adopters and eventually a receptive market."

Ann Ting, Confer's co-founder and Chief Technology Officer said, "In retrospect, the Confer product was a superb technology. Confer participated in a competitive sale to the Palo Alto Medical Foundation, a large integrated delivery system in California. They were in the market for a patient medical records system. At the end of the evaluation, it came down to two vendors, Confer and Epic Systems. At that time, Epic was the EMR market leader and a firm who had been around for many years. Confer had only been around for two years. At the end of the process, the Foundation said Confer was functionally head and shoulders above Epic. However, the conservative hospital IT administrators did not dare take such a big risk on a young company and instead chose Epic."

At the end of the day, Mayfield Fund, a staunch supporter of Confer, believed it would need to raise significant new capital to buy the time required to succeed. Bill Unger said, "We needed to find hospital administrators that wanted to be better at delivering care. All our due diligence indicated the practitioners wanted this. Our failure was understanding the economics of the healthcare IT marketplace." Confer misread the institutional power structure at hospitals. The power base did not reside in the hands of the doctors and nurses Confer focused on. Instead, it resided with IT and administration. In the end, the decision on what software platform to purchase was made by the hospital's administrators. To Confer's great disappointment, these administrators were not ready to move the state-of-the-art forward.

While seeing the promise of the Confer technology, the broader venture community read the same tea leaves. Despite outreach from Mayfield, no one would step up with adequate new capital to help keep the company afloat. Out of necessity, the Board chose to sell the business to another software company in June 2001 at a price well below what they hoped for.

Had Confer been able to survive long enough, it's possible the market could have caught up with the company's vision. Today we see some small signs of this kind of continuous care chain management starting to emerge in some larger, more sophisticated practices around the country. Dr. Ting continues to receive further affirmation of Confer's ultimate importance and value. When recently doing a patent search, she came across multiple filings citing Confer's intellectual property portfolio as prior art from organizations looking to build process and resource management applications to meet the evolving needs of payers and providers.

For Confer as an ongoing entity, it was not to be. Confer had an accurate vision of where the market needed to go, and it had the right product to get it there. But the company was ahead of its time. Confer was a textbook case of bad market timing on the early side. The product they brought to market was superior to the competition in virtually every way. However, the elements of the opportunity, particularly a more practitioner- and patient-focused view of care delivery, simply were not in place. Confer may have been in the right place, but they were there at the wrong time.

Chapter Fifteen

Surf the Next Wave

Winter was around the corner as Josh Kanner made his way towards Davis Square in Somerville, Massachusetts. It was early in the evening just after Thanksgiving, the sun had set, and festive Christmas lights decorated the trees along the street. As Josh turned the corner onto Elm Street, he saw the distinctive black and red motif of his destination for the evening.

Located in the heart of Davis Square, The Burren is an authentic Irish Pub with a worn wooden bar featuring a wide array of beers and whiskeys. In the back of the pub, a small stage and dance floor hosts local bands to entertain the crowd and accompany the lively dancing. On a typical evening, young professionals and graduate students from Harvard, MIT and Tufts pack into The Burren.

As Josh entered the pub, he wasn't sure what kind of discussion to expect. Looking around the crowded bar, he spied Adam Omansky sitting at a corner table towards the back of the room. Although Josh didn't realize it until later, the conversation he was about to have with Adam would impact his life for years to come.

Josh and Adam met for the first time earlier that year on a ski trip set up by a close mutual friend. During the trip, Adam learned with interest of Josh's background in the software industry. Now several months later, Adam's motive for meeting with Josh that evening was to discuss an idea for a potential new software product.

Adam opened their conversation in the crowded pub with a story about a paper he wrote while at the Harvard Graduate School of Design. Having studied architecture and project management during his academic years at Cornell and Harvard, Adam spent the prior ten years working on commercial real estate projects. While working on a Four Seasons Hotel project in Budapest, he ran into a common problem faced during construction projects. The flow of information between the field and all of the project stakeholders could easily take days to filter throughout the organization. This bottleneck in information flow produced delays, resulting in construction projects missing key deadlines. What's more, he spent thousands of dollars for software to equip his office, but there was no software available to capture and communicate critical field information. His Harvard paper focused on an approach to solve this problem.

Adam knew a lot about construction. He didn't know much about software. And, that's why he reached out to Josh. After explaining the problem and providing a brief glimpse into a solution, Adam asked Josh if working together on this concept might interest him. The idea intrigued Josh, and he agreed to think about it.

At the time of their initial meeting, Josh was Director of Product Management at an enterprise software company in the Boston area. As employee number eleven, Josh witnessed the explosive growth of the company. Initially responsible for product marketing, Josh's role grew over time to include guiding product strategy. Five years after joining Emptoris, the company was over 250 employees serving over 100 customers. Looking back on those days, Josh recalls, "Being part of a rapidly growing company can be exhilarating. I loved working with customers, our engineering and sales teams to build new products that changed the way work was done. In the back of my mind, I knew I wanted to get back to building something from scratch. That's where all the fun is."

After their initial meeting at The Burren, Josh and Adam started working nights and weekends to explore their software idea. The core concept behind Adam's idea was a collaboration tool to address the communications gap between the construction site and key decision makers. They wanted to build a platform containing all the planning data used by building owners, contractors and architects. This platform would provide greater visibility into a construction project to improve communications, help minimize delays, and reduce cost overruns.

Over the winter, "Using only Powerpoint, we built a non-working prototype for the application," said Josh. "We shared our design with John Macomber, who was one of Adam's professors at Harvard. We received positive feedback from John and a few other folks we reached out to. So, we knew we were onto something." By April 2005, enough positive feedback had piled up. "I had my 'holy shit' moment that this couldn't be a nights and weekends gig anymore," said Josh. A few days later Josh quit his job and co-founded Vela Systems with Adam.

Vela Systems combined Josh's background in enterprise software alongside Adam's background in construction management. This union of product expertise blended with market expertise is crucial in the early days of a startup. Josh knew they had the makings of a strong team, but he quickly learned where Adam and he were weak. "We knew what we were doing in the product and customer side of the company," said Josh. "But, we didn't know anything about raising capital to launch the business. We would talk to anyone who would listen. After many months of conversations over a beer or coffee, our initial investment finally arrived in January 2006 from a ragtag crew of angel investors."

Any startup company CEO will tell you how challenging it is to raise financing and build a business at the same time. It's a difficult juggling act. Josh had to ask himself, "Do I spend more time raising capital or do I spend more time talking to potential customers and helping build our product?" By the summer of 2006, Josh had accomplished much on both of these goals. His team delivered a first release of their product and signed up some early, marquee customers. And, in addition to the initial angel investment in January, he was able to close a much larger round of just over $1 million.

The new financing came from Launchpad Venture Group and Common Angels, two of Boston's largest angel groups. Along with the funding, both angel groups placed one individual on Vela's board of directors. In the case of Launchpad, Tim Curran was the ideal candidate for a board seat. Tim was an experienced software company CEO. At the time of the Vela investment, Tim recalls, "I had just sold my previous company to Trimble and I was looking for something new. When I first met Josh and Adam, I let them know I had experience building software applications. I had nothing to do at the time, so I offered to help them out. Taking a board seat put me in an ideal position to work closely with them."

Vela Systems was the first company where Tim held a non-management board seat. "I didn't know if I was doing a good job, since this role was so new to me," said Tim. "But, I had many years of experience as a CEO, and I could pass along my learnings to Josh. After board meetings, I would spend the rest of the day at the company to help out and coach Josh and his team."

Over the next year, Josh and Tim built a strong working relationship and began to understand each other's strengths. "As we started the process of raising a new round of financing," said Josh, "it became obvious to me that the best way to maximize the value of the company was to make Tim the CEO. I was always calling Tim for help. He had relevant experience building an enterprise software company. By making Tim the CEO, he could help raise our next round of financing. I could stay focused on making our product the best-in-market. The transition to Tim as our leader was one of the three biggest value-increasing inflection points for the company."

During the period from 2007 through 2009, the team at Vela Systems worked hard to deliver on Adam's vision of bridging the information gap from the activities in the field to the owners, architects, builders and project managers on large construction projects. Their initial product was hard to use. "We were trying to deliver an easy-to-use mobile experience for our clients," said Josh. "But, the capabilities of mobile devices hampered us at that time. Our software ran on tablet PCs, which were expensive, heavy, and had a short battery life. The adoption rate of our product was slower than we planned and we weren't growing as fast as our investors expected."

Wouldn't it be great if you had the ability to predict the future? If you knew in advance which path led to success, wouldn't you choose it every time? Well, in February 2010, something like that happened at Vela. "I was in my office reviewing our sales pipeline, when in walked Daniel Cozza and Pete Billante," said Tim. "We hired Daniel the year before as our Chief Technology Officer. And Pete had been with us for about three years as our VP of Product Management. I could tell from their demeanor as they sat down this was going to be a serious discussion."

Tim said, "Daniel launched into a two part pitch. For his first point, Daniel explained to me why we needed to halt development on our current Windows tablet PC platform. He said our current path was a dead end. If we continued down the tablet PC path, we might as well shut down the company, and he would quit. Given our poor track record of recent sales, I agreed we had a problem. And, I sure didn't want to lose Daniel. But, what would we use as a replacement technology platform?"

Tim said, "That's when Daniel hit me with part two of his pitch. He asked if I was aware of Apple's new tablet called the iPad. Daniel explained how he had a pre-release of Apple's software and had built a prototype of the Vela application. He further explained the iPad would solve many of our current tablet PC platform problems. The new device was light weight, had a full day of battery life, had a cellular modem, and cost about a quarter the price of a tablet PC."

Tim couldn't help but acknowledge the logic in Daniel's two part pitch. Tim supported Daniel's efforts to convince Vela's management team and their board. It wasn't an easy decision for the company to make. Abandoning the platform all your customers were already using, and forcing them to waste tens, if not hundreds of thousands of dollars on recently purchased tablet PCs upset quite a few Vela customers. Even though Tim and his team didn't have a crystal ball to peer into the future, they knew, deep down, moving to the iPad was the correct decision. Tim secured the board's approval and gave Daniel the go ahead to abandon tablet PCs for the iPad. Two months later, Vela Systems released its product as an app on the iPad App Store the same day Apple shipped its first iPad to paying customers.

Vela's timing on its move to the iPad was critical to the company's ultimate success. Yes, you could say there was some luck in the team's decision, and you would be partly correct. There were no guarantees the iPad would be so successful. Yet, Daniel and Pete had the vision to see the importance of this new type of mobile device. Furthermore, they understood mobile's broad impact on the delivery of technology to everyone in the near future.

More than three years in advance of the introduction of the iPad, Josh Kanner had the foresight to build business relationships with key partners in the construction technology industry. From his time at Emptoris, Josh learned the value of partnering with industry leaders.

When Vela launched its first product in 2006, Autodesk was already one of the two big gorillas in the construction technology market. Their industry leading products, AutoCAD and Revit, were in use by millions of architects and builders around the world. Most of Vela's early customers were also customers of Autodesk. So, they were an obvious candidate for Josh to focus his partnership efforts upon. Josh leveraged Vela's customers to help establish a strong working relationship with Autodesk.

Josh met regularly with key executives at Autodesk. He knew building lasting relationships would take significant time and effort on his part. And, he knew as he spent the time, he would learn more about where Autodesk faced serious challenges and issues of their own. Thinking back on some of his interactions with Autodesk, Josh said, "The construction industry is about relationships and passion for making a change, whether as a customer or tech provider. I wound up becoming close friends with my partner contacts at Autodesk, bonding over a shared desire to change the industry. Our conversations over mutual customer meetings, dinners and late night drinks provided me with the insight to understand what they really needed from Vela Systems." What Josh discovered during those late night dinners proved to be incredibly helpful as Vela strengthened its relationship with Autodesk.

The iPad version of Vela's product was an early success. It highlighted Vela's prowess in delivering a quality mobile application. Furthermore, Vela stored all client data on remote computers based in the cloud. This use of a cloud architecture was critical for their large, international customers. These customers could now access their construction data from any device, anywhere in the world. Today, that doesn't sound so impressive, but in 2010 that was a huge technical breakthrough.

Vela's technology direction lined up perfectly with what Josh discovered during his conversations with Autodesk. "By 2011, during my meetings at Autodesk, I kept hearing their desire to move into three areas," said Josh. "It was clear to me that mobile, cloud and social were three areas where they wanted to develop deeper capabilities. We didn't have social, but we were pioneers in mobile and cloud for the construction industry. Our move in 2010 to the iPad and the cloud was perfectly timed."

Towards the end of 2011, Autodesk made their first offer to acquire Vela Systems. Vela's board rejected the initial offer as too low given the value they brought to Autodesk. Driving Autodesk into an acceptable valuation zone required significant negotiation. Over the ensuing nine months, Autodesk presented two additional offers to purchase Vela. Suffice it to say that Josh and Tim can look back and smile at the stories of those negotiations.

In the end, they received a substantial offer from Autodesk, which they accepted. Both parties did well. Vela's employees and investors walked away with a solid payday for the company they had built. Autodesk acquired a product and a team that pushed them into the modern world of mobile and cloud computing. At the time of the acquisition, Autodesk was worth $6 billion. Over the next seven years, their market cap grew seven times greater. And, you could easily argue Vela played a key role in that growth, as then CEO Carl Bass mentioned Vela as "the fastest growing product acquisition in the history of the company" in back-to-back earnings calls. In 2019 Autodesk has made construction technology a major emphasis for the company with additional acquisitions. Their stock has continued to rise. Everyone won.

Vela's success is a story about choosing the right path at just the right time. You could argue the iPad saved Vela. Without an inexpensive, highly capable mobile device, Vela would never truly satisfy their customers' needs.

Just as important as getting the timing of a move right, is being able to see where the future is going and make that move in the right direction. Daniel and Pete had a deep conviction that the tablet PC would not be a viable platform for Vela. Furthermore, they were willing to bet early on the iPad and the cloud as the correct technical path for Vela to follow. Josh was able to support their technical conviction with insight he gained in frequent discussions with Autodesk and other companies in the construction technology industry.

A window opened for Vela Systems in 2011 in the form of a technology platform shift, and they had the foresight to go through that window. Initially eluding them, the building block technologies finally came into place to allow them to deliver on Adam Omansky's vision from way back in 2005. Yes, luck was involved, but they worked hard to position the company to take advantage of it. And when the time came, Autodesk realized they needed Vela.

Chapter Sixteen

Build For Tomorrow, Not Yesterday

It was the summer of 2007, and all appeared calm on the horizon. The US was in the fifth year of an economic expansion, the housing market was booming, and consumer confidence was at historically high levels. It looked like a perfect time to set out on an entrepreneurial voyage. So it was with great enthusiasm and optimism, Pete Eggleston, Elio Maggini, and Christopher Payne-Taylor took a leap of faith and launched their startup, AdME (Advertiser driven Mobile Engagement). The company was going to help major brands increase engagement with their customers.

The most talented economists, technologists and futurists couldn't have predicted the fierce challenges Pete and his team would encounter over the next two years. Like the maritime disaster detailed in Sebastian Junger's *The Perfect Storm*, Pete would confront the confluence of two powerful economic weather fronts and a major technology hurricane. Unlike the crew of the doomed fishing boat *Andrea Gail*, Pete and his team lived through their perfect storm and are around today to tell the tale of their startup company, AdME.

Pete's life course was destined for an entrepreneurial career. As a boy, Pete ran the largest paper route in town. He later got involved in door to door selling, first with a mail-order seed selling business, then others in an attempt to scale up orders. By the time he was ready for college, he was interested in technology and earned a bachelors degree in electrical engineering from Stony Brook and a masters degree in computer science from the Rochester Institute of Technology.

In his first job after college, Pete discovered he had the skills and the drive to succeed at sales. Even though he trained as an engineer, his natural sales talent blossomed when he interacted with customers to uncover, then help solve their biggest problems. With an innate ability to listen to customers and undertake market research, he found he had an ability to 'engineer' successful product and marketing strategies. Over an eighteen year period, Pete applied his talents to senior management roles at Amerinex Applied Imaging, Plexus and Sonic Networks (later rebranded SoniVox).

During those early years of his career, Pete never lost his entrepreneurial spirit. All three companies were relatively small when he started out with them. Through them, he learned much about running a successful startup.

Pete joined Sonic Networks in 2003 as Vice President of Sales and Marketing. At the time, Sonic developed sophisticated music engines for cell phones and mp3 players. Pete's job was to license this technology to major companies throughout the US, Asia and Europe. Sonic was incredibly successful with their music engine, and Pete was able to close deals with many of the leading cell phone and sound chip companies. In addition to the cell phone companies, Sonic signed a major licensing agreement with Google. This agreement moved the Sonic music engine technology into the public domain and allowed Google to embed the Sonic music engine into the Android mobile phone operating system.

If you played video games in the mid-2000s, chances are you were one of the many million fans of the music oriented titles

Guitar Hero or *Dance Dance Revolution.* These games were megahits in the rhythm and dance video game genre. Played in family rooms, basements and video arcades all over the world, the games became a cultural phenomenon that generated billions of dollars in sales.

In 2005, when Guitar Hero was first released, many of Sonic's customers asked Pete if his company could develop a similar game for their cell phones. According to Pete, "The idea intrigued us, and we wanted to take advantage of this huge new market for rhythm and dance games. We put together a small game development team and started the development of a new game platform."

The initial concept behind the platform was to build a developer's tool to simplify the creation of rhythm and dance games for cell phones as well as other mobile devices. With the recent success of *Guitar Hero*, and the explosive growth of cell phone usage, building cell phone versions of the game was an irresistibly intriguing possibility for the team at Sonic. Pete reached out to Harmonix, the publisher of *Guitar Hero*, and Sonic negotiated a license with the company to develop a cell phone version of their game.

By 2007, Google recognized the importance of Sonic's music engine for their Android operating system. They struck a deal with Sonic to acquire the music technology. A change in ownership of this technology resulted in big changes for the company, for Pete, and for his team.

"Jennifer Hruska, Sonic's President, asked to meet with me and discuss what my plans were for our new game platform," said Pete. "At the time, we were struggling to complete the software. But, interest in what we were doing was high. AT&T was offering us encouragement and willing to help launch our first games. As one of the top two cell phone networks in the US, this was a big deal for us."

Over the next few months, Pete sifted through what the Google acquisition meant for him and his future. He realized he had some difficult decisions to make, but also an opportunity to take some initiative. "The big question in my mind was do I take a risk and do something new and entrepreneurial," said Pete. "I thought a lot about it and also talked to my colleagues, Elio and Christopher. We had numerous conversations and planning sessions where we discussed whether there was a real market and real customers to support our game platform concept."

In Pete's view any new business had to have a very solid foundation. "We didn't want to create a startup company just for the sake of saying we did it. We needed a high level of confidence that we would succeed. Of course, there is no sure thing with startups. You can never be 100% confident. But our gut told us the timing was right and the opportunity was real. After some negotiations, we agreed to spin off the game platform from Sonic into a new company, which we named AdME. I worked out a deal with Jennifer where I would continue to sell products for Sonic on a part time basis to provide cash flow to bootstrap the company, and they would license the game platform to our fledgling startup."

Building applications for cell phones was very cumbersome in the mid-2000s era. To help developers do it at scale, AdME was going to have to overcome some important technical barriers imposed by the realities of cell phones. Back in the pre-iPhone days, there were significant differences between cell phones. An application written for one phone would be useless on the others. Application developers had to port their applications to each new phone. The complexity for developers became overwhelming as more and more phones were released to the mobile market.

Pete and his team believed AdME had an elegant solution to this formidable barrier. "We built a platform that eliminated all coding for game developers," said Pete. "Our initial platform came with two game play styles. One was similar to *Guitar Hero* and allowed game players to simulate playing a guitar. The other was a variation on *Dance Dance Revolution* where players dance to a beat based on patterns presented on the phone screen."

Using the AdME platform, a game designer could customize the look-and-feel of their application with images and logos of their choosing. So a major brand like Burger King could build a custom app using their marketing content. These fun-to-play music games would act as an advertisement for their brand and keep their customers engaged. They didn't have to write any code. They didn't have to port their application to hundreds of cell phones. And, they didn't have to endure the onerous game certification programs dictated by each carrier. The AdME platform took care of all that.

What could possibly go wrong?

One of the biggest challenges faced by startup companies going after a new market is the sales cycle. This cycle includes the time and resources needed to educate customers. In AdME's case, their target customers were primarily large brands such as technology companies like Motorola, entertainment companies like Atlantic Records and ABC, and consumer goods companies like Wrigley. In the process of speaking with the marketing departments at these large brands, Pete quickly learned he would need to work with their advertising agencies, as well.

"I knew technology and I knew selling, but this was my first introduction to the world of advertising. I had a lot to learn," said Pete. "Since AdME's platform helped brands create what was essentially a new form of advertising, I needed to position what we did as an experiment. What I found out along the way was brands valued both exposure and engagement with their target customers. If I could show how our games would increase customer engagement with a brand, we were onto something big."

Many of Pete's preliminary conversations with brands and their agencies were very encouraging. "The concept of applying cell phone games to improve brand engagement made them sit up and listen. Not spending a lot of time educating them on the potential surprised me," said Pete. "It was pretty quick to get them engaged in the idea and they seemed to get it. At the time, it made me think it would be easier to sell to them than it ended up being." While Pete thought he saw clear blue skies all around, in reality storm clouds were starting to build.

During the Spring of 2008, Pete and his team were making steady progress building their product and speaking with prospective customers. They were able to raise a few hundred thousand dollars of seed capital from angel investors in Boston. Things were looking up... until they weren't.

The leading edge of a major economic weather front was fast approaching that Spring. The AdME team was totally unprepared for the onslaught they were about to face. The Great Recession of 2008 was one of the most difficult financial periods we had faced in modern history. There were more than 400 US bank failures during the ensuing four years. The stock market plunged by almost 50% from its peak in July 2007 to its low in March 2009.

The economic recession had a massive and immediate impact on AdME. In Pete's recollection, it was not pretty. "My first indication that we might be in trouble happened during a discussion with a potential investor. One of Sonic's early investors indicated a strong interest in making an investment at the time we spun out from Sonic. When I reminded him of his interest and asked him about writing a check in 2008, his response was not what I expected. A few years earlier, on the advice of his financial advisor, he invested in Mortgage Backed Securities. Little did he know that these 'safe' investments would become ground zero in the current financial crisis. His savings were decimated and he didn't have any investment capital to risk with a startup company."

Lack of liquidity spread throughout the financial markets and many angel investors started to slow down their investment pace. They kept some dry powder to help existing investments stay afloat, but investing in a new startup didn't interest them. Pete's potential sources of capital to support his business were rapidly drying up.

Another impact from the economic recession appeared during Pete's meetings with the brands and agencies who were to become AdME's customers. There is a negative impact on advertising budgets for consumer brands during any major economic downturn. CFOs are always looking for places to cut back on company expenses during tough times. Unfortunately for AdME, marketing budgets were a great place to start.

Since AdME's approach to brand engagement was unproven, agencies and companies considered their approach to be an experiment. During good economic times, a brand's VP of Marketing might allocate 10% of the marketing budget to try out new things. In 2007, when AdME was getting off the ground, times were good, gaming and mobile were hot, and AdME was a likely candidate for experimental marketing dollars. By the middle of 2008, companies slashed their marketing budgets right and left, with the experimental budgets being the first to go. Pete became deeply concerned his only source of revenue was disappearing fast.

As the calendar turned to 2009, AdME's financial picture looked pretty grim. Lack of new investors and customers with no experimental marketing budgets placed Pete in a difficult bind. His two sources of working capital, equity investment and customer revenue, completely disappeared.

To compound AdME's financial problems, a major technology wave appeared out of nowhere when Apple introduced the iPhone. The iPhone was a radical departure in terms of mobile computing platforms. By 2008, it was clear it was going to have a huge impact.

Pete didn't miss the early indicators that the iPhone would change everything. Yet, he couldn't fully appreciate just how significant the iPhone would turn out to be. Elio Maggini, AdME's CTO, ran a quick experiment to see how much effort it would take to build their product on the iPhone. It was a relatively straightforward effort. AdME would need to support another mobile phone along with all the other phones they were already supporting. But, Pete didn't think he had the resources to take on another phone. And, it would require a pivot in their business plan, something he did not feel would sit well with the investors.

Furthermore, agencies and brands weren't asking for the iPhone at the start of 2008. According to Pete, "When I called and asked if we should pivot to the iPhone, all I heard was no. However, six months later during the Summer of 2008, agencies started calling me and said they wanted the iPhone. All of a sudden the dialogue I was having with them switched from what do you have on feature phones to what do you have on the iPhone? Even though feature phones were still the majority of the market, in hindsight, I should have pivoted to the iPhone at that point in time."

Could a faster embrace of the iPhone have been AdME's savior? That's a difficult question to answer today. It took a long time for the economy, and ad budgets, to recover. And, it's doubtful the company could raise the necessary capital from investors to keep their lights on during that time of scarce revenue. Additionally, iPhone iOS and Google's Android platform were ushering in a smartphone revolution with a completely new era of application development for mobile devices. Gone were the days of fussy ports to multiple devices. Now developers could write for two platforms and reduce their porting efforts by several orders of magnitude. This fact alone eliminated one of AdME's biggest value propositions, the ease of building gaming apps for all phones.

Brands and their agencies never embraced AdME's concept of customized games to help increase brand engagement. So it is not clear that the initial traction which Pete thought he uncovered during the early days of AdME was anything more than a fleeting fad with limited staying power.

By the Spring of 2009, the handwriting was on the wall. Pete could no longer bootstrap the company and keep the team together with no cash in the bank. He had to accept the fact his timing on launching AdME was unlucky. No one predicted the Great Recession, and Pete was not to blame for his inability to properly finance the company. However, he does accept responsibility for missing the impact of the iPhone on AdME's business. A strong economy would've kept AdME alive, but the iPhone would've decimated AdME's core value proposition to their customers.

Pete started the process of finding a buyer for the company's technology assets. He thought he could find a software company interested in their platform, but there wasn't any interest in the company's assets. Although the storm had passed and there was blue sky peeking out, there was destruction everywhere. It was time to declare an end to the AdME story.

Pete took it hard and felt he let his team and his investors down. But in July 2009, Pete recalls speaking to one of his investors from whom he got a refreshing piece of advice, "Pete, get on with your life and I will write off my investment." Most angel investors understand the risks they take when they invest in an early stage company. Although we don't like to take a loss, we know it's futile to try and keep a company alive when it is facing a Perfect Storm.

Chapter Seventeen

Late Comers Need To Stand Out

Before investing in a startup company, early stage investors constantly ask a key question, "Are enough customers ready and willing to try this new product or service?" Ken Rainin, an inspiring serial entrepreneur, successfully confronted this "Is our customer ready?" question time and time again.

Ken was an extraordinary businessman and charismatic leader. He was the type of person one was drawn to, high energy, grounded, funny, and with great business instincts.

Ken graduated from The Ohio State University with a degree in English. After a brief stint as an industry salesperson, Ken founded and built Rainin Research, a developer and manufacturer of scientific instrumentation. The company is best known for its invention of the automated pipette system found in most scientific research laboratories.

As CEO of the company, Ken demonstrated vision every step of the way. He understood the laboratory instrument market, what it needed, and how to package, position, price and deliver products to the customer. These skills, combined with his uncanny instincts for product positioning, made Ken a great leader. He bootstrapped Rainin Research until it's acquisition by Mettler-Toledo in 2001 for $290 million.

During his time running Rainin Research, Ken was also an active angel investor. At the suggestion of his brother, a practicing ophthalmologist, Ken helped found and finance a company called Ioptex. Ioptex designed, manufactured and sold intraocular lenses. These lenses are surgical implants used to replace the natural lens when it becomes a cataract. As we age, the eye's natural lens becomes cloudy. A cataract forms reducing our ability to see clearly. To correct cataracts there is a short surgical procedure, where an artificial lens replaces the natural lens. This procedure accounts for a significant percentage of Medicare dollars spent in the United States.

Ken had to confront two big challenges with Ioptex. The first challenge was all about timing. The company was a late entrant in a crowded market. Major competitors included Johnson and Johnson, 3M, and Abbott Medical Optics, among others. Ken's second challenge was with Ioptex's products. While safe and clinically effective, their products were not highly differentiated. Many competitors offered similar products.

Furthermore, Ioptex faced additional hurdles, including a limited product offering, little or no ability to buy market share, and limited working capital, as Ken had personally financed the company. Hiring skilled sales representatives and key executives was also a challenge. Talented performers were reluctant to join an unproven, poorly financed, late market entrant.

So how was Ken going to overcome the challenges that would doom most less experienced entrepreneurs? Ken knew he was going to need a clever way to differentiate his product if he was going to succeed. He thought deeply about his market moment, and he thought empathetically about where his customers were at. Decades of new but expensive technological advances were forcing physicians to make investments in both technology and skills in order to stay competitive in their market. This left them little time to manage their practices during a period of increasing competition. Ken's winning insight was to understand these issues, and to time delivery of a solution for its problems perfectly.

Working closely with its sales organization, the company cleverly formulated a novel and unique sales approach. This unconventional approach would prove to be the key to penetrating the market and ultimately drive the company's success. Tom Smith, an early Ioptex sales representative in San Francisco, recalls why he joined the company, "I recognized Ioptex's novel selling process to the market could be a potential game changer."

Tom said, "I called this process value-add selling, providing the customer more than the device itself. Years ago, service stations sold gas. Today, they sell service, sundries and other items to meet the customers' needs, hence value-added selling." Tom believed this creative sales approach could help Ioptex overcome other barriers to success in this highly competitive market.

Ken hired Jim Rybicki to lead the sales effort and further develop the value-add sales approach. Jim championed the emerging Ioptex sales strategy. He recognized and appreciated the extent to which physicians, in addition to their clinical practice, were managers of small businesses, roles for which they had no training. Ken's insight was that these physicians needed more than a product. They needed help. Ken believed the Ioptex representative could provide this support.

Tom said "On a sales call we didn't talk just about our product's features and benefits. Our sales calls were built around strong working relationships with targeted, pre-qualified physicians, and introducing them to our value-add practice development tools." The typical Ioptex representative, said Tom, "Worked to fulfill the customer's specific professional needs which may have nothing to do with the device we were trying to sell."

Ioptex created a suite of practice development tools. These tools offered the overwhelmed physician a chance to grow both financially and professionally. The Ioptex sales approach got them in the practice door and kept them there.

This sales methodology was transformational because it was not merely transactional. Transactional selling, the industry standard, is tactical in nature. The salesperson focuses on features, benefits and price. Transformational selling begins with understanding the customer's real needs. Tom began sales calls by asking open ended questions. What are your objectives for the practice? Where do you want to be in five years? Do you have a strategic plan to help get there? The questions focused on the practice, not the product he was selling. In closing, he tells the physician, "I think we can help."

This customer-first attitude built strong professional relationships, and broke down normal barriers to entry in most practices. The Ioptex representative would spend far more time with a physician, who wanted to discuss the business of being a physician, than competitors would spend. The sales rep was there to deliver common sense advice to the physician.

Given their customer-first orientation, it was only a matter of time before the company gained a foothold in practices and developed a loyal and growing customer base. This was a win-win strategy. The practice worked better, the patient flow increased, and as a result Ioptex sold more of its lenses. Competitors found the Ioptex strategy mystifying and were completely unable to emulate it. Whatever barriers existed due to Ioptex's late timing into an already crowded market were overcome by its novel, game-changing sales strategy.

Understanding the company's potential, Ken knew the next phase of growth entailed broadening their market opportunity by selling to more mainstream customers. He recognized in order to do so he needed cash, and this was more cash than he was willing to personally put at risk. Coincidentally, in the summer of 1986, bankers took note of Ioptex's growth and suggested Ken consider taking Ioptex public. Eager to make some money from his investment in Ioptex, Ken agreed. For a number of reasons, the public offering failed. One of the core reasons was timing.

Just as the company was getting ready to market the deal, the stock market had turned south. During the pre IPO roadshow, the stock market suffered a precipitous one-day fall. The stock market cooled. The only way to complete the offering, said the bankers, was to reduce the price. Ken refused and started looking for alternative financing.

The timing wasn't right for an IPO, but Bob Stockman, an ambitious, young investment banker contacted Ken and proposed to organize a leveraged buyout of a significant piece of Ken's ownership in the company. Supported by Merrill Lynch Interfunding, the deal closed. In doing the deal, Ken fixed his liquidity challenge but replaced it with a debt challenge. Sales and high margin growth were critical. Cash was king. Paying down debt was a key objective.

Ken hired Joe Mandato to walk this financial tightrope as the Chief Operating Officer for Ioptex. Joe's broad and deep ophthalmic industry experience impressed Ken. He was still running Rainin Research, so he counted on Joe to develop the company's infrastructure, especially in marketing, strategy, and operations.

One of the first things Joe did after joining Ioptex was to work with his team to formulate a strategic plan for growing the business. At the core of this effort was a desire to better define the ideal target customers, the customers who would respond best to their value-added sales approach. They had to make sure Ioptex was well positioned as a valued partner not only to current customers, but to a large enough number of future customers. This would ensure continued customer stability, loyalty and growth.

The new management team sought to codify what was working about their new sales approach so they could hire and train additional sales reps capable of practicing it. The team spent time in the field with Ioptex sales professionals, including a rep named Kevin McMahon in Upstate New York. Using the value-add approach, Kevin developed a small but productive customer base. "In physician visits," Kevin said, "I made simple suggestions. I recommended the office staff be uniformly dressed and wear name tags. I stocked the office with patient education materials. I suggested the practice throw out months old magazines and order new subscriptions. They loved me for what I could do for the practice. I was a smarter rep than the competitors. I charged nothing for my thinking. It was my way of being a professional the physicians valued. Value-add selling worked."

While Kevin's suggestions may seem obvious, they weren't to many of the physicians. Time and time again, physicians told Ioptex that the changes the company representative recommended increased patient satisfaction immediately. Patients of Ioptex's trained physicians noted the practice offered a better patient experience in an attractive, patient-centric office. Physicians also noted their satisfied patients generated new patient referrals to the practice.

With a deeper knowledge of their market moment and their target customer in hand, the Ioptex management team sharpened their focus on training their salesforce. Deep down they knew they had to grow a highly consultative sales team able to do what Kevin did in New York. To pay off all their debt, the company's primary challenge was to accelerate high margin growth by expanding their customer base. And consultative selling was the chosen path to success.

Joe said, "It was critical for us to identify and hire quality sales reps according to our well defined, customer-centric selling approach. We looked for customer-centric sensitivity as a key indicator to help us hire new sales professionals. The rep's ability to understand and master the Ioptex practice development tools was a key element to our success with customers and prospects."

Joe also spent his early days at the company trying to understand what the company could not do. First off, it couldn't match the industry's focus on market share, which stressed features, benefits and price. Joe said, "The industry's focus on market share was a war we could not win. Our goal was to grow in high potential territories with physicians who fit our profile. We needed fewer, more productive practices to grow and succeed."

With a strategic plan in hand, Joe's team was ready to execute. They identified their ideal target client as young ambitious surgeons who were early in their career and looking to build a new generation of medical practice. These surgeons were looking to grow and develop successful businesses while enhancing their own images as future key opinion leaders. Mark Hayward, the company's first marketing director said, "Through careful research, we were able to identify the practices where we should focus our attention."

By methodically expanding what worked in their high growth accounts, they used their practice development sales approach to drive further growth. Seeking board approval for the plan, Joe described the target physician customer to the board. He said, "Being a competent surgeon is no longer sufficient to succeed in a competitive marketplace. The surgeon-owner of the practice needed to understand how to best drive and manage a business." Further, he said "It's necessary for the physician to be a marketeer, a businessperson, a lawyer and a manager, all at the cost of time doing surgery." Recognition of the importance of these issues and a focus on solving them was key to Ioptex's success in expanding its business.

The company enhanced its practice development offering to include more sophisticated materials. The company refined and built upon the simple tools Kevin McMahon offered. Sales veteran Tom Chirillo said, "We added a layer of sophistication, which was a powerful draw for new customers and difficult for competitors to copy." Some of the new components in their offering included: staff education, patient education, marketing, reimbursement, patient productivity flow, and patient referral networks. All of this was designed to attract new patients for the physician.

With a well defined target customer profile and great sales tools in place, the final piece to the puzzle was recruiting and training a top notch sales team. As a start, the company identified and targeted two well regarded industry sales leaders. Each of these sales reps had a large and seemingly loyal customer base. Ioptex convinced the reps it would provide an opportunity to grow professionally, through its consultative sales strategy. It took some training and a shift of mental attitude, but within a year the new reps successfully converted a high percentage of their current business and began closing new business. These high visibility reps brought Ioptex credibility when approaching other high performing reps. With that, Ioptex was off to the races.

So were enough customers ready and willing to try this new product or service? Ioptex made sure they were the answer to this question in the ophthalmic market. The company understood the market moment and customer's needs better than the competition. It provided non-traditional tools delivered by a knowledgeable sales rep to meet the needs of growing practices. The company's handbook, *Strategic Planning for the Ophthalmic Practice*, included a detailed evaluation of the practice, and a potential strategy and plan to achieve the practice objectives.

Ioptex's revenue growth continued as its customers increased productivity and increased surgical volumes from their current and expanding patient base. And, as new Ioptex reps approached cash flow breakeven, the company hired more reps from a full pipeline of prospects. Great salespeople wanted to be with a winning team.

Were customers ready for the Ioptex lenses? Yes, but the company's insight was that they were ready for more than just a good product. Ioptex's recognition that their customer base was also looking for the sales representatives' advice and counsel was a game changing insight. Employing a value-add strategy using practice development tools produced results.

Ioptex was ultimately acquired by Smith & Nephew, a British healthcare company. Despite competition from large entrenched competitors, Ioptex had grown to number four in market share. Its compound annual revenue consistently grew in excess of sixty percent despite being in a slowing market with eroding prices. It grew by successfully taking share from the competition. Ioptex became the industry's most profitable company. It maintained the industry high average realized price, while fanatically managing its expenses and paying down debt. Ioptex's market timing in rolling out a new approach based on understanding what customers needed and how to best meet those needs was the winning formula.

Theme Five

Will Your Company Be Bought or Sold?

"Your Network is Your Net Worth."

Porter Gale

Chapter Eighteen

First, Get Noticed

As General Counsel and later, CFO, at IONA Technologies, Christopher Mirabile gained a wide breadth of experience with mergers and acquisitions. Although this work was in a large company context, the insights he gained serve as a valuable lesson for smaller startups hoping to make it to the big leagues.

Christopher remembers the environment and characters vividly. "Meetings with corporate development VP Tom Davidson always took forever. Not because of Tom. He got right to the point. It was because of the interruptions. Tom was an incredibly busy and in demand guy. He ran the corporate development function at IONA during the 2000's. I remember Tom's undecorated office on the top floor of IONA's US headquarters in a leafy suburb of Boston. The office was close to the exact center of the building, located not far from the water cooler and was always a hub of activity.

When things were busy, meetings with Tom didn't have a beginning or an end. They were just interludes in a stream of interruptions. Christopher said, "One day I went to see Tom to discuss acquiring a company that was already one of our sales partners. We were looking to fill a gap in our product line. Based on commercial dealings, we knew the partner's team were people we trusted. And, the technology was robust enough to serve the needs of our customers. Tom and I needed to discuss the most discreet way to approach a company with whom we already had regular business interactions across various business functions."

Given the broad scope of platforms and product functionality a middleware integration company like IONA had to cover, and the security and performance required, corporate development activities were essential to maintain a competitive product offering. It was a simple fact of life that acquiring other companies in their market was often necessary to meet the rapidly evolving needs of their broad and demanding customer base.

"The partner Tom and I were meeting to discuss that day had not been the first company we considered for this deal. But the original acquisition target reached out to was not a fit," said Christopher. "A couple of IONA's engineers liked the original target's technology and thought it could be integrated into their product. But the target company was small. It was not well known to us or our customers, and the product was largely unproven. Acquiring them might plug a technology hole, but their unrecognizable name and unknown capabilities would do nothing to reassure customers that our product was being paired up with the best in the market."

Tom's work was directly connected to the needs of the business. He did not sit around daydreaming of interesting companies he might buy. Nor did he set out with a blank sheet of paper to research terrific companies. He was driven by the needs of his colleagues, and those colleagues were driven by the demands of the market. In Christopher's view, "When things were boiled down, there were only two drivers of the deals Tom did. The first driver was corporate strategic planning. This planning focused on assessments of where the market was going and what technology the company needed to address those changes. The second driver came from product managers demanding help in order to meet competitive pressures. These pressures were in response to complaints from the sales force when they lost deals."

Despite receiving a continuous stream of inbound inquiries from companies looking to be acquired, those inbounds never set the agenda. Christopher said, "Everything Tom did was predicated around responding to actual or anticipated competitive pressures. Unsolicited inbounds didn't give rise to any of our acquisitions. What gave rise to acquisitions was exigent circumstances. This might include specific companies stealing IONA's sales with better features or performance, or competitive moves which threatened to redefine the market if not met with a response." If you were an ambitious little startup in this market waiting to be acquired, you were like the kid playing pickup basketball waiting to be discovered. Tom was not going to come find you without a good reason.

The particular deal Tom and Christopher were working on that day came about because sales people were losing sales and were squawking to the product managers. Product management in turn looked at the typical 'buy vs. build vs. partner' analysis. In this case, product management agreed the problem was real and felt time was of the essence. Engineering did not have the cycles to take the project on right away. An acquisition became the best path to address lost sales.

Christopher said, "Once it becomes clear it's time to make an acquisition, the best candidates are usually right under everyone's noses. The most obvious starting place is the company causing all the market disruption." But that company is sometimes not for sale on reasonable terms. At IONA, in situations where the obvious candidate was either impossible to acquire or a bad fit, the corporate development department would turn to other companies on their radar screen.

What does it mean to be on a company's radar screen? Simply put, market relevance or personal connections. It might be a company the sales team partnered with. It might be a competitor giving the marketing team fits. It might be a company someone met while doing a panel at a conference. Or it might be a company employing an engineer's colleague from a previous job. But whatever its nature, there is always some kind of connection to drive the necessary awareness.

Because corporate development happens in a maelstrom of competing priorities (e.g. ongoing deals, incoming requests, integration of past acquisitions,) there is rarely, if ever, any time or appetite to do a top-to-bottom market assessment of a group of small companies no one has heard of. The reality is, if the company is not already known and making some waves in the marketplace, it has little chance of being acquired by a strategic buyer. What is the lesson for startups in all this? "Put simply," Christopher said, "corporate development professionals are busy. They are not going to come find you. If you want to get acquired, there are really only two ways to do it. You can carve out a market position which is a threat to a potential acquirer, or you can build connections within the class of potential acquirers."

In this theme we look at the stories of four companies which illustrate the deliberate efforts needed to make an exit happen. Sometimes, investors and the board of directors need to guide, and perhaps, force the CEO to sell the business. Other times, it's the CEO who drives the process by constantly reaching out and making connections to potential acquirers of the business. No matter the situation exits won't happen without dedicated effort.

If you don't have the kind of technology that is threatening, and you are not big enough to put a dent in your market, you are very unlikely to be discovered. You have no other choice but to build the connections within the potential acquirers necessary to familiarize them with what you do and where you plan to go. And you have got to maintain those connections to keep yourself on their radar screen and top of mind. It's that simple. You either need to make a splash in your market, or make friends on the playground. Otherwise, you are just shooting baskets in your driveway, waiting for the NBA to call."

Chapter Nineteen

Get Out While You Can

Moving and thinking fast are a way of life for Steve Skillings. Irreverent, and quick to make a joke, Steve has silver-flecked hair that contrasts with his lanky frame and youthful demeanor. He's a whip-smart engineer and self described nerdy car guy. He's also a guitar player, passionate about music. In the late morning on a Saturday in February 2008, this go-fast car guy was bombing down the left lane of a Massachusetts highway. He was mentally chewing on a challenging problem as he approached a long stretch where the highway went under some buildings. As he entered the dark shadows under the hulking concrete structure, the solution was still eluding him. By the time he emerged back into the sunlight, he not only had the solution to the problem, he had the core of his future startup's business plan.

Steve grew up in Maine and describes himself as, "The kid who could take anything apart and put it back together, no problem." A first generation college student, he studied engineering at Clarkson University, a well respected program on an often frigid campus, nineteen miles from the Canadian border in northern upstate New York. Given his mechanical proclivities, Steve was a natural to study mechanical engineering. And Steve had a fascination with business, so he minored in business administration. Recalling his motivation, Steve said, "In engineering you like solving problems. And the biggest, most convoluted, multivariable problem I've ever come across is business. Just when you think you understand it, external things happen to you, and all of a sudden all of your formulas are not working as before. You have to reinvent things that were once reliable."

Right out of college Steve managed to combine engineering with his love of cars by taking a job as a product development engineer with Gates Corporation, a large manufacturer and major supplier of automotive components to the industry giants. As a management trainee, Steve quickly moved through product development, sales engineering, tooling, and account management, learning as he went. Before long, despite rising through the management ranks at Gates, Steve was ready for something new. He and his wife Marci were ready to get out of Gates' factory in the small city of Auburn, Maine, and try a new part of the country. Steve took a job at a design and engineering firm in Portland, Oregon. He and his wife packed up and moved to the Pacific Northwest.

Even with a demanding client load, Steve wanted to push his business skills further. With his typical self deprecating humor, Steve recalls those difficult years, "I was working at the design firm, and because I'm a complete idiot, I decided it was time to get my MBA. I was working sixty hours a week, helping with a baby, and I was taking classes at night. By the time I graduated, we had two young kids in the house. I guess that's the curse and blessing of being someone who likes to stay busy."

Having young kids reinforced the pull of family. So after five years in Portland, Marci and Steve decided to return to the East Coast. They chose Massachusetts to be nearer to their children's grandparents. Job selection was a bit more serendipitous. Steve recalls looking up at the sleek white ceiling speakers in his MBA classroom and thinking about how cool it would be to work for their maker, the Bose Corporation. The drive to move east took on a new dimension when Steve realized Bose was located near family, in Framingham, Massachusetts. Steve applied to Bose and was hired as an engineering manager for the audio component maker. He was to start in Bose's automotive division, which would allow him to combine both cars and music into one dream job. Steve and Marci packed up and moved back across the country.

Bose is where Steve came into his own as a manager, and, later, as an entrepreneur. His resume accurately describes him as an intrapreneur for Bose. Steve developed a reputation as an innovator and trouble shooter who would not hesitate to point out a problem then dive in to fix it. This brash pragmatism earned him a place on the fast track, but it was not always easy. Recalling awkward management situations, Steve winces. "I was willing to say, 'This shit's broken and it's not helping our business. Why are we doing it?' That approach doesn't always resonate inside of a big company. But you've got to be willing to say 'this is the elephant in the room nobody's talking about.' I'm willing to put it out there. I think that's why I did well at Bose."

As Steve's rising star status and seniority grew, so did his entrepreneurial drive. At times that drive conflicted with traditional career paths. When exposed to some experimental technology Bose was working on for live music amplification, Steve had a passionate gut level reaction. "One day my boss comes in and says 'you're a guitar player, right?' I said yes. He says 'there's this incredible new speaker that Bose is developing for musicians.' So I go and get a demo. My jaw is on the floor. The sound quality was theoretically impossible."

That was on a Wednesday. By Sunday of that week, Steve decided to leave his senior management posting with Bose's fast growing eCommerce group to join this live music project. "I couldn't stop thinking about it. So on Monday I go meet with the guy who is running the project. I tell him I have to work on this. I'll do anything you need." The manager said he had no openings but Steve said, "I'll do customer support. I'll do whatever you need. I have to be a part of this." The next day the manager called Steve up and said, "We made you an opening."

Steve became the fourth person on the team. At this point Steve was following his passion and his transformation into an entrepreneur was nearing completion. It was a seemingly crazy move. "I left behind a staff of eighty in the corporate world. All my colleagues said, 'You're way up in the company. Joining this crazy little group in a tiny little market is career suicide.'" Steve, who was seized more by his passion than his pragmatism, was unmoved. "For an entrepreneur, it is about solving problems and driving forward. That's a much bigger driver for the entrepreneur than status. I jumped in with both feet."

The evolution from intrapreneur at Bose to entrepreneur running his own company started, oddly enough, on the sideline of his son's soccer game. It was a bright, crisp, colorful fall day. A fellow parent was describing the challenges his son was having finding band practice time at their condominium complex. Steve's first thought was that the neighbors must be good sports to let them practice at all. But, what he blurted out was how sad it was that a kid with musical passion could only practice two to three hours a month.

This really bothered Steve, and it was still bothering him on the highway on his way home as he went under that overpass. The solution that occurred to him during those fleeting overpass shadows was the world's first silent rehearsal studio for musicians. Steve's vision was to build a console that members of a band could plug their electric instruments into. The console would allow musicians to blend their collective sound so each could hear a perfect mix of the band on headphones.

Steve was certain he could build it, and was told that it could solve one of the biggest problems in music retailing. Steve said, "I was told once, 'The industry was good at building tennis racquets and bad at providing tennis courts. This could be our tennis court fix.'" You cannot sell instruments if people don't have a place to play them. Steve's JamHub device would open up a whole new world of silent practice spaces for the industry.

As soon as Steve had his highway epiphany, he was obsessed with it. "It's crazy. I go straight home and I run past my wife. She is yelling 'What are you doing? How was the soccer game?' I tear upstairs to my home office, grabbing an engineering pad and a pen. I start sketching the product and diagramming the electrical schematic. Before that weekend ended, I had most of the engineering, market data and most of the business plan." Steve was soon out of Bose on his own and into the treacherous world of startups where the entrepreneur's dreams and interests for his products aren't the only ones that have to be considered.

Hardware startups like JamHub are difficult because they require significant amounts of capital. You need capital to build and refine prototypes, set up manufacturing, create and maintain inventory, and find distributors and retail space. After getting things off the ground with savings and some important support from friends and family investors, Steve knew he needed to seek out more professional angel investors to provide additional working capital.

With professional investors come complications. Steve's JamHub startup was no different. Right out of the gate the company's situation tested the new investors' patience. A massive recession hit at the end of 2008, just a few months after closing his $1.1 million preferred stock seed angel round. Starting with incredible promise and industry accolades, the company booked $3M in orders in its first eighteen months. But due to the recession, it soon found itself awash in returned, unsold inventory. As the recession deepened, it became clear the high build price and resulting retail price point of this non-essential hobbyist device was going to be a problem. Distributors and retailers began slashing orders and returning previously purchased units.

In the face of slower than expected hardware sales, Steve accelerated the company's software plans, and began casting about for additional investors to keep the company afloat. Steve's software vision was bold. He envisioned a cloud-based recording and editing platform called BandLab that featured support for multitrack recordings from the JamHub unit, and powerful social features for collaboration and discovery. Bold though the software vision was, it did little to assuage the anxiety of his angel investors who were already badly shaken by the sales reversals and thinking about how they were going to get out of this company whole.

Steve's search for more capital led him to follow up with an Asia-based investor who was the son of a very successful industrialist. The investor, whom we'll give the pseudonym Bayu due to the requirement to protect his privacy, learned of the product at a music industry conference. He immediately saw huge potential in the BandLab product. Bayu seemed to have nearly limitless resources and wanted to make a very significant investment in the company.

Faced with the prospect of this infusion of fresh capital, existing angel investors felt a mixture of relief and concern. They felt relief because the company was going to have badly needed resources. But they felt concern because of the significant ownership dilution the deal would create and because of the extent of control Bayu wanted. These angels felt they had seen this movie before and began asking Steve whether it was possible to be bought out as part of the deal. Steve was in no position to press for that since he did not want to send the wrong message to Bayu. The company needed the money for working capital purposes rather than to fund secondary sales by shareholders. The angels had little choice but to agree to the deal.

The experience was very eye opening for Steve. He was still passionate and enthusiastic about the company, but his angel investors were scared. This was Steve's first tangible lesson about the need to drive your company not just for success, but for a good exit outcome for your investors. Until that moment he had an operator's mentality. He was focused on the day-to-day process of running the company. The angel investors' expectations were an attention grabbing reminder of his overall goal for the company.

Soon after making the initial investment, Bayu suggested the company move its software efforts to Asia. This seemed logical to all involved, but it soon became clear there were downsides, at least for the angel investors. Bayu ramped up the software effort and it rapidly consumed the company's resources. Bayu was willing to provide more money, but naturally required more ownership in the company in return. Given the company's rising expenses, Bayu was the only investor willing to put more money in. He was effectively in the driver's seat. When the angel investors took stock of the situation, they again asked Steve if he could come up with a way to protect them from steady dilution straight into oblivion.

Steve and the company's board knew if they were going to take care of their investors, including friends, family and dozens of angels, they were going to have to intervene and try to make something happen. After much analysis, the board proposed splitting up the company. Bayu would take 75% of the BandLab software business, and early investors would take the hardware business and inventory, plus retain a 25% stake in BandLab. The assumption at the time was the investors could sell off the existing JamHub hardware inventory for operating cash flow while they sought a buyer who could acquire the entire business and return cash to all the investors.

The first problem was the inventory did not sell. The economy was weak and the hardware operating unit had minimal working capital to rebuild sales, marketing and channel relationships. Further, Steve was pulled in two directions, having to travel back and forth to Asia working as CEO of the software business while simultaneously working to sell the hardware business.

Board members Carla Grillo and John Paulos, who had been elected by the angels at the time of investment to represent the interests of the angel investors, knew they had to step in and help facilitate an outcome that worked for the angels. Carla was a former Wall Street investment banker who had been at a global tier one bank. Initially, confidence was high that a deal could be found for the company that would monetize the inventory and recoup the value of the product brand and design.

Working with a consultant hired by the company, Carla used her connections to make a number of introductions to find a buyer for the struggling business. Months were spent trying to find someone interested in the company and its aging inventory. The more people Carla talked to, the clearer it was that the hardware business was not going to be a source of liquidity to pay back all the investors. An offer for the business was not forthcoming. Eventually the decision was made to shut it down, and investor focus turned to the 25% stake in the software business as a last Hail Mary play.

Part of the reason for the renewed focus on the ownership stake in the software business was the spectacular media attention the company was receiving for having purchased 50% of one of the most famous and long-standing magazines in the music and entertainment industry. This purchase was an example of the significant money and effort expended to develop and bolster the BandLab social network. The angel investors started to regain a little hope that their rapidly diluting, but still significant stake might someday be worth something. But, by that point, both the friends and family investors and the angel investors were completely passive investors. They had little say in the business beyond Steve's continued seat on the BandLab board.

Steve did his best to represent the investors, but the company was moving quickly. It was just one of many projects Bayu had on his plate. Under Bayu's leadership, the board did not meet at all, nor was adequate financial or operating information being provided to investors despite multiple requests. Further, Steve was conflicted due to his ongoing management role.

It was clear to Carla and John, the original board members, that they were going to have to find a path to liquidity for the company's angel investors. The solution was to appoint Carla, with her investment banking background, to take Steve's board seat on the BandLab board. Since Carla was not constrained by the duality required in Steve's management role, and had a life-time of experience dealing with tricky corporate situations, she was able to put significant governance pressure on Bayu and the BandLab team.

This level of accountability was not easy or comfortable for someone like Bayu, but Carla kept the pressure up, knowing it was the only way to safeguard the interests of the investors. Before long, the awkwardness of the situation drove the BandLab team to broach the subject of a buyout of the remaining shares. The problem was, Bayu was not in a position to pay the kind of money it would take to reimburse both the angels and the friends and family investors. Because the angels held preferred stock and the friends and family investors held common stock, the angels were first in line. This led to an incredibly difficult situation for Steve.

First of all, he was not convinced it was the right time to sell the stake. He was closer to the business and thought it had the potential to be a big winner. But he understood the angels desire to cash out and move on. He felt a professional obligation to his angel investors who had provided the capital to grow the company. But he also felt a personal obligation to the friends and family who had believed in him and provided funds when the company was just an idea.

In deference to the wishes of his investors, Steve reluctantly embraced the idea of selling and explored every option he could to find a way to cover everyone. But Bayu had already put a ton of money into the business and was not looking to pay more to buy out the remaining stake. After months of negotiation, Steve made the agonizing decision to accept BandLab's best offer. Given their preferred share priority, the angels got their money back and a small additional return. But there was not enough to cover all of the friends and family investors. Steve could not let that stand, however, so he used some of the proceeds from selling his own personal common stock to boost the pool for common stock shareholders.

The angels were delighted to walk away with a modest 17% return, but Steve struggled with the outcome. He said, "I was accustomed to doing great things my whole career. This was a good outcome, but it wasn't great. Good is not what I am accustomed to doing." But with time to reflect, Steve came to appreciate the perspective that it wasn't just about him. "Investors are in the boat with you. Sometimes you've got to do what's best for the boat as a whole, not what you want. The professional investors have absorbed a lot of losses in their career, so they may be incredibly happy with a merely good outcome. I guess you have to find your joy in that. You can't let perfect be the enemy of good enough." Carla Grillo recalls the same motivations. "It was difficult, but the angel investors were so happy at the end. That is why I stayed on the board for six years. I was not going to have my name associated with something that was not a good outcome for the investors I represented."

In retrospect, this was a difficult business launched at the worst possible time, immediately before a major recession. The product was solid, and the team was talented. But the company struggled to find its footing, and got into a complicated situation with a strategic investor. In situations like that, investors cannot just sit at home and wait for an exit and a check in the mail. Exits don't just happen, they have to be created. In this case, Steve's fierce drive to protect his friends, family and early investors, combined with coaching, assistance and intervention from his entire board, was the key to staying in the batter's box and swinging until he got a hit for his early backers.

Chapter Twenty

Making the Exit a Top Priority

When pitching to investors, many entrepreneurs get overzealous with their exit strategy, spending too much time on what might be, and not focusing enough on the practicalities of bringing their vision to market. After all, exits aren't a possibility without working product and a functioning business. In certain situations, however, a proactive, explicit exit strategy is what the entrepreneur and board require as a condition of going forward. Such was the case with Loma Vista Medical.

Loma Vista was a medical device company led by Alex Tilson, a high energy, skilled engineer in his first founder/CEO role. Under his leadership, Loma Vista had a couple early strikeouts and had run very low on money. When he went out to seek more, the investors were very clear. They were not going to back this first timer any further, unless they were convinced there was a viable pathway all the way to exit.

Alex founded Loma Vista in April 2006 after having enjoyed a broad set of engineering experiences in several high tech medical device companies. Just prior to his tenure at Loma Vista, Alex was looking to grow as a leader and manager and took a position as Director of Engineering at InSound Medical, a company partially financed by De Novo Ventures, a Palo Alto, California venture firm. At the time of the initial investment, Joe Mandato, a general partner at De Novo, became Chairman of the InSound board. Joe helped with the recruitment and hiring of Alex.

During Alex's tenure as Director of Engineering at InSound, the company went through a number of product development challenges in what was a politically charged atmosphere. And, as time went on, the company also experienced a number of formidable operational challenges. Though Alex was both skilled and competent, the Board eventually asked him to leave the company. Joe agreed with the decision as both Chairman and lead investor.

This began a very difficult period for Alex. Coming out of his experience at InSound, his instinct was to start out on his own. After some careful consideration, and with his family's support, he decided to start his own company. When asked why he decided to found a company at this point in his career, Alex's response was clear, "I was ready. It's as if I'd been training to do so all my career. I was comfortable leaving a company and starting something of my own. Of course, it helped that InSound fired me," he added with a smile. While a risky decision, Joe Mandato, Alex's former chairman, commented, "It was the right move for Alex and the timing made sense. He learned what he needed to learn to launch a startup, and he was well suited for the entrepreneurial lifestyle."

At Loma Vista, Alex began working on an innovative system to perform colonoscopies, a procedure performed many millions of times around the world. At the time of Loma Vista's founding, Alex recognized colonoscopy devices had seen minimal innovation over many years. Only a few large Japanese companies produced these devices. The market leader enjoyed 75% market share. He knew it was a solid, established market ripe for innovation and perhaps disruption.

Alex bootstrapped Loma Vista, but before long, raised funds from friends and family. He intended to manage Loma Vista based on the popular lean startup model, a framework built upon the belief that spending less is more. Unfortunately for Alex, the lean model may be more appropriate for a software company, where prototypes are created within 24 hours at little cost. In contrast, Alex was producing a new, sophisticated piece of hardware requiring much engineering and rigorous testing in a compliance driven environment subject to FDA approval.

All of these steps were difficult, costly and time intensive. Additional resources were clearly required. Given the degree of financial risk to him and his family, the lean approach needed modification if he hoped to have a reasonable chance of success. Alex said, "Medical devices often involve novel materials, sophisticated or even new manufacturing processes, with many design iterations. All of this would extend timelines. We couldn't be capital constrained. Financing was critical to mitigate risk and time to market. So we modified the lean model to a prudent but lean model"

So, Alex set out to raise more money from his existing friends and family, angels, small funds and family offices. He was reluctant to approach traditional venture capital funds simply because there was an inherent conflict between Alex's lean approach and the traditional VC model which dictated that venture funds deploy enough capital for their winners to move the needle on fund returns.

Alex did approach one fund, De Novo Ventures. Alex reasoned the team knew him well enough to understand why his tenure at Insound Medical was so brief. Alex said, "Joe hired me at Insound. In addition, I knew his partner Jay Watkins." Alex was betting a recognized fund like De Novo could bring his project credibility when approaching other investors.

Although Joe agreed with the decision to fire Alex from Insound, his view of him was positive. He said, "Alex is a good person, but more importantly, he is a passionate, demanding, focused engineer who maintains high standards for himself and his team. In the right environment, Alex could blossom as a leader and succeed as an entrepreneur."

De Novo supported Alex with a $200,000 investment in Loma Vista. Although a modest investment for a VC, De Novo was still able to own a substantial stake in the company. And with two board seats, De Novo could closely monitor the company's progress and influence management thinking when needed. With the money, Alex and his investors hoped Loma Vista's product development effort would accelerate and reduce the company's time to success. Unfortunately, that was not the case.

About ten weeks after De Novo's investment, Alex's team hit a product development roadblock. The product did not work as expected. Most early generation disruptive products need multiple iterations. This came as no surprise to the investors. However, in Alex's mind there was no remedy to the product's deficiencies. He had tried to no avail. While the fundamental engineering principles remained valid, the device failure was due to an unanticipated and insurmountable negative interaction between the device and the tissue it was meant to navigate.

Supported by his team, Alex made the difficult decision to halt development and regroup as a company. Alex would later say, "Successful people are really persistent. They'll beat their heads against the wall again and again, and that can lead to a real breakthrough. But, sometimes being successful is about having an understanding of when it might be necessary to move on."

Alex was not defeated. He had some money left. With the remaining funds, Alex huddled his team, took stock of the company's capabilities, and tried to plan a future. Coming out of those deliberations, the team concluded they were good at working with novel materials to produce medical inflatables - devices utilizing air pressure to change shape after insertion into the body. What they needed was to quickly identify a specific product and market to enter. And they had to prove they could build it. Otherwise, their investors might call it a day and fold the company.

After careful study, they concluded the first potential application of their new inflatable technology platform could be an existing, high volume spine procedure, balloon kyphoplasty. It was a large, fast growing market with one major player, Kyphon, a division of Medtronic. Medtronic had recently acquired Kyphon for close to $4 billion, lending credibility to Loma Vista's projected product value.

Alex decided his company would go ahead and propose a pivot to the new business strategy, while leveraging its prior learning and core technology. Alex knew pivoting a company like this was a legitimate strategy, but it was not common in medical devices. It was fraught with risk, and would require additional funds. The key question for Alex was: how would his investors react?

"Pivoting," Joe said, "was not often seen in the life sciences. However, I knew it was doable. As with everything he does, Alex did a deep and thorough analysis to demonstrate to me and my partner, Jay, that the proposed pivot was not only doable but, given the circumstances, a smart and pragmatic change of strategy and direction."

The team cleverly planned to leverage existing assets. They proposed a new and innovative materials science product platform which could eventually be put to use in multiple applications beyond kyphoplasty. The board agreed with Alex's new approach, and led a modest $1.1 million round with existing investors. Alex, once again, began to execute the plan. Within twelve months, his team built a product superior to that of the market leader.

Right as Loma Vista reached its product development goals and began their commercialization efforts in 2012, the kyphoplasty market suffered a significant downturn. A leading medical journal challenged the efficacy of the procedure against traditional treatments. The ensuing debate was loud and costly and caused significant industry headwinds. A new, small startup company was in no position to weather this storm. Loma Vista had a serious problem.

Moving quickly, Alex proposed a second pivot as yet another means to find a market for their materials expertise and drive an exit for investors who were again confronting the very real risk of company failure. And for lead investors Joe and Jay, their credibility and judgement in steadfastly supporting Alex and the company could legitimately be challenged by their partners and other investors. Compounding the challenge was Loma Vista's need to raise yet more funding should it choose to pursue this second pivot. While still modest, DeNovo's investment had grown. The partners had to consider the opportunity costs of maintaining and extending their support of Loma Vista. The question before them was, "Is this the time for investors to throw in the towel, or could they find a way to achieve even a modest return for investors?"

The new pivot was to focus the company on the nascent but growing heart valve replacement procedure. This was a potentially exciting market, but at the time it had a relatively modest total addressable size. Alex took his usual deeply analytical approach when broaching the subject with investors. According to Joe, "Alex came to De Novo with in depth research demonstrating multiple examples of successful and pretty dramatic pivots by other companies. The list was extensive, and a fascinating read. For example, Alex pointed out that the blockbuster drug Viagra was originally designed to treat hypertension, when users noted an obvious side effect. He also felt the percutaneous heart valve market was ready for growth and would provide multiple opportunities for exit."

So it was time to make a choice. They could either embrace or reject another pivot. Things were uncomfortable, but there were key differences in this proposed plan relative to the previous pivot. Certain board members, especially Chuck Love and

Joe's partner Jay Watkins, had a deep understanding of this heart valve market.

Jay had served as head of business development at one of the world's leading cardiovascular companies, Guidant Corporation. Chuck spent many years working in the cardiovascular market. Furthermore, Chuck and Jay had long standing relationships with key industry leaders and potential strategic partners. These connections could, and ultimately did, prove vital in helping Alex get to know the key industry players.

The proposed Loma Vista product would be a key accessory for a pioneering procedure. The product enabled a surgeon to perform heart valve replacement surgery through a small incision, without having to penetrate the chest wall as required by the then current standard of care. This type of surgery was a small, emerging, yet fast growing market with enormous potential. The tool Alex wanted to develop would simplify the procedure and lead to less trauma for the patient. The key to the tool was a flexible composite balloon which would inflate after being inserted through a small incision to provide access to the repair site. By removing significant surgical risk and effort, this new product reduced costs and recovery time. Alex believed it might very well accelerate the growth of the heart valve replacement market. Importantly, the Loma Vista team knew the target market was squarely in the sight of multiple large medical device companies, all of whom were potential acquirers. Several of these companies could ill afford having the Loma Vista product get in their competitors' hands.

The team felt they had a strong value proposition and wanted to move forward. Their product provided the surgeon a tool to perform a faster, less traumatic procedure, one much easier for the patient to tolerate. They would position the product in the heart valve marketplace with new and powerful messaging, "The True Balloon - Truly Precise, Truly Tough, Truly Fast, Truly Better." For surgeons and for industry leaders, the positioning statement seemed to say it all in an accurate and meaningful way.

Alex met with his board. Once the board had time to absorb the new idea and the scope of opportunity it represented, there was enthusiastic support for his proposed pivot. Of course, courage and confidence in the pivot were enhanced by the reality that the alternative was to close the company.

However, patience was wearing thin. After nearly four years, the company had raised meaningful funds, approximately $3.5 million. To move forward, the board encouraged Alex to focus resources on building to an exit. They directed him to engage early and often with industry leaders to test and validate the company's thinking and to engage the board in this process. The board was aware that while the company had been floundering, the device market had changed. Jay Watkins commented to the board, "There is carnage out there. Companies are dying, getting nothing. It is a tough market, but I believe we can make something happen here."

The board challenged Alex and his team to: 1) determine how much money they needed to get the product done, 2) get the product into the market on a limited basis to prove its efficacy, and 3) get to an expeditious and financially attractive exit. The board didn't give Alex an open ended invitation to build a big company. Rather they instructed him to build a salable asset.

Given the board's mandate, Alex proceeded without delay. The new money helped to complete product development and design an efficient, scalable manufacturing process. Joe said, "After four years of effort, it felt like we were putting lipstick on a pig. In other words, Loma needed to look good. The company had limited capital to reach key milestones and we needed everything to work when potential acquirers came calling."

As soon as Alex refocused the company on the heart valve market, he began reaching out to potential partners and acquirers, introduced to him by his well connected board. By the end of the process, he had spoken with fifteen different companies. From the discussions, it was clear that several of these companies looked at the product not only as an opportunity, but also as a potential threat if a competitor acquired the technology. It was those vulnerable companies on which Alex focused his effort. Other potential acquirers took a lower priority, including the market leader who, while not dismissive, clearly suffered from a 'not invented here' syndrome.

It was a long, exhausting process. But Alex was determined to make it happen. Loma Vista received three offers, all from companies in the threat/opportunity category. The board felt that any of the offers could be the basis of a solid transaction. After much back and forth, the company reached an agreement with CR Bard, a large and respected public company.

The board knew it had the best offer it was going to receive, but it came down to Alex and what he wanted to do. The board knew they could not sell the company without the CEO's support of the deal. This was Alex's first experience as an entrepreneur, a CEO and company leader. He hated to give that up and walk away. But he felt loyalty and gratitude toward his investors and to the team who helped him reach this point. Alex said, "I have seen things crumble, and I always vowed to take something reasonable and not be too greedy, particularly as a first time entrepreneur."

Alex knew an attempt to hold out and increase shareholder value would be very high risk and involve the investment of a lot more time and money. The immediate offer would be a very good financial outcome and investors would be rewarded with a nice return on their capital. Alex wisely chose to take the deal.

Alex is on to his next startup, a different man, a wiser man and of course, a wealthier man. The Loma Vista experience was a classic case of the board pushing management to focus its activities on what was necessary to drive an exit, which at that time, was essential. Key board members dedicated their time to providing Alex guidance and counsel. Alex focused on the critical tasks needed to deliver a financial return to his investors. This included opening doors to key decision makers in major companies in the industry segment as well as sage and engaged counsel on the entire negotiation process. The end result was an expeditious and successful exit. Part of Alex was tempted to hold out for more. But, with coaching he came to understand the importance of not letting perfect be the enemy of good.

Chapter Twenty One

Potential Partners - Trust but Verify

"There are only so many IPO candidates out there. I invest to make a return. If the entrepreneur or I can't put our finger on obvious alternatives to an IPO, something is wrong," said Ron Conway, one of San Francisco's most prolific and successful early stage investors. Ron has been an active angel investor for over twenty years, investing early in companies such as Google, PayPal and Facebook. So, you can surmise he knows a thing or two about making successful investments.

Given his focus on exits, one of the critical success factors Ron uses when evaluating a new investment is whether the entrepreneur knows the universe of potential buyers. And, knowing everything there is to know about these buyers, as we shall see, is a critical element for driving a successful financial return for a company's founders and investors.

This brings us to the story of a company called InSound Medical (yes, the same InSound Medical where Alex Tilson of Loma Vista served a stormy term as Director of Engineering). The founders of InSound were passionate entrepreneurs focused on improving the lives of the large and growing segment of our population with a hearing impairment. The number of people in this segment is staggering. Millions of individuals collectively spend billions of dollars every year on some form of hearing aid.

But, it's a crowded market with many companies selling a wide range of hearing aids. When InSound launched its first product, there were already several well-established market leaders trying to differentiate themselves from one another and be the device of choice for new purchasers.

As to Ron Conway's point about knowing potential acquirers, there were many for InSound. All of the market leaders kept a watchful eye on any new products entering the hearing loss market. In fact, several of these bigger companies expressed strong interest in acquiring InSound throughout the company's history. As we all know, however, nothing is simple. Despite interest from multiple parties, there were circumstances beyond the company's control that drove the timing of InSound's exit and its choice of acquirer. The outcome was somewhat positive for investors but it could have been substantially improved had InSound better understood its buyers and if it had the luxury of controlling its own exit timeline.

Adnan Shennib, an experienced industry engineer, and Dr. Robert Schindler, a highly respected Ear, Nose and Throat specialist at the University of California San Francisco founded InSound Medical. The company was initially funded by several deep pocketed angel investors, none of whom had hearing industry experience.

The founders' vision, which early investors endorsed, was to build a large, successful, industry leading company that addressed one of the biggest issues affecting hearing aid adoption. A key market objection to wearing hearing devices is their visibility, which can drive perception that the wearer is old or infirm.

Enter the Lyric, the world's first invisible hearing aid. It is invisible because of its small size and could be manually placed by a hearing professional deep in the hearing canal, adjacent to the eardrum. The Lyric's design allows customers to wear the device continuously for as many as 120 days. It is a disposable device that does not require battery changes. And, in a survey, 96% of users preferred Lyric over other devices they used in the past.

InSound's product development pathway was no different from that of many early stage companies. It was a long, costly and rocky one. The company tended to release each version of its product before it was ready, and in the process, burned through large sums of capital going from fix to fix.

Initially, InSound's co-founder, engineer Adnan Shennib, led the company. He focused his fundraising on angel money and priced each round higher than the last round without regard to the market realistic valuation the company deserved. As a result, subsequent institutional financings became challenging, costly and dilutive to early investors. The early angel investors developed short tempers as the value of their holding diminished. One key investor, Ken Rainin said, "I have completely lost trust in the company and its management." As the largest investor, Ken's attitude influenced other angels as they considered investing. As angel feedback trended negative, the company needed to rethink its fundraising strategy. A decision was made by the board to reach out to the venture capital community.

Two venture firms, Psilos Ventures and CMEA, agreed to co-lead an investment into InSound. De Novo Ventures and Johnson & Johnson's venture arm both joined as new investors. The round was substantial with $25 million added to the company's coffer. The company's financial plan indicated this would be enough funding to get their product all the way to market launch. Rod Altman, the partner in charge of the CMEA investment, when asked about his motivation to invest said, "The product was truly disruptive, it met many customer objections to current offerings, and the market is huge." If successful, InSound could turn the hearing industry upside down. Rod added, "There was no product remotely like InSound's long lasting, deep in the ear canal, invisible hearing aid."

Before finalizing their investment, the VC syndicate believed the company needed change. First, it needed an experienced, disciplined CEO. They were looking for someone who could effectively lead the company to a successful product launch, and ultimately, a sale of the company.

Second, the company needed a clearer exit strategy. The founders' objective was to build a standalone company. However, new investors wanted an opportunity to exit, when appropriate, via acquisition. The industry was lacking in truly meaningful innovation and there were a number of potential acquirers competing on modest feature improvements, benefits and price. Finally, InSound needed to restructure its board with cooler heads and applicable industry expertise.

Following a CEO search, the company hired David Thrower to run the business. He was an ideal candidate. David was a Stanford graduate with a degree in mathematical and computational sciences and a Harvard MBA. He had experience in the hearing aid industry as VP of Global Marketing at GN Resound, and had also served as VP of Marketing for Align Technology, the developer of Invisalign invisible braces.

David checked all the boxes. He had experience marketing hybrid medical/consumer devices directly to the consumer. He knew how to overcome the resistance of the clinical customer to adopt new, disruptive technologies. And, he understood the hearing market and its key players. David's motivation was clear, "It was a chance to be a CEO. I loved leadership, strategy, and driving cross-functional problem solving. Being a CEO allowed me to do all three in an industry I know."

After taking the helm at InSound, David spent significant time and money overcoming a number of continuing product performance challenges, hiring key members of his leadership team, reducing costs, and building a sales organization. He led the company to a successful launch, ending year one at a $10 million dollar revenue run rate. It was a strong beginning. But, it also accelerated the need for expansion capital on top of the $70 million raised in prior rounds of financing.

In 2009, David and his team drafted a plan to raise additional capital. The business was growing and he wanted to accelerate that growth. The economy, however, got in the way. With the stock market in freefall at that point in time, early-stage venture backed companies had limited access to funding. Furthermore, healthcare focused venture funds lost their identity and their station in the Silicon Valley ecosystem. They avoided what they perceived to be early, unproven opportunities, including In-Sound. Frustrated with the pace of fundraising and unwilling to put in more of their own money, the board advised David to consider strategic alternatives.

The Lyric hearing aid was gaining market traction, and In-Sound was starting to attract attention from bigger companies. Rod Altman said, "David had done a good job of getting in front of industry leaders. Interest in the company surfaced and that interest provoked more interest." Rod added, "Then, out of nowhere, Siemens, an industry leader, announced that it was getting out of the hearing aid business. It was a shock to InSound and the loss of a key potential partner."

Given the state of the economy, the hearing aid industry, and the near term need for cash, the board advised David to begin a formal process to sell the company. They hired Gravitas Healthcare, a small investment banking firm, to assist in the process.

Gravitas reached out to a universe of ten or more traditional and less traditional potential acquirers. Two European companies, both industry leaders, emerged from the process expressing serious interest. The two contenders were Phonak, the market leader based in Switzerland, and Oticon, a large Danish company. In both cases, InSound was a logical potential acquisition to fill a corporate technology gap. Neither company had a product to attack 40% of the market dissatisfied with current offerings.

Gravitas was able to create a moderately competitive bidding process between Phonak and Oticon. However, companies in the hearing industry aren't known for having aggressive acquisition strategies. So a bidding frenzy was not in the cards. An exacerbating factor was that these were conservative European companies. European device companies tend to be slow, methodic, and careful buyers. And, they tend to not overpay.

The bankers at Gravitas pushed the competing parties. After much back and forth, Phonak invited InSound's CEO and chairman to a face-to-face meeting in Los Angeles. The meeting's objective, they said, was to negotiate a deal.

The meeting was a disappointment. It went on for several hours replete with nonstop posturing and exaggeration. In the end, Phonak proposed a lowball offer for InSound, amounting to approximately 20% of what ended up as the final transaction price. As CEO, it was clear to David that the company was not communicating its value properly and that it had more work to do. David said, "The offer demonstrated they clearly did not appreciate the strategic value of InSound and did not view it as a potentially disruptive product."

So why was the initial offer so low? Was it based on a traditional multiple of sales calculation? Perhaps the bidder believed InSound had no other offer? Or, given InSound's modest sales, was Phonak interested in its intellectual property to keep it from competitors? David continued, "They were there to buy what they thought was an unproven asset, interesting IP, at a bargain price." They were not there to aggressively acquire a strategically critical or disruptive technology, nor to develop a long term and trusting relationship with InSound's leadership.

But, according to Rod Altman, the VC from CMEA, "We had our backs to the wall, we needed to get something done." So, the discussions continued, albeit at a snail's pace. The bankers, aggressively supported by management, kept both potential acquirers engaged. They effectively negotiated between the two until InSound and Phonak reached a mutually acceptable price.

For InSound, the purchase price included a so-called earnout component. With an earnout, some of the purchase price is paid over time when and if certain milestones are met. An earnout allows the seller to capture a higher price based on superior performance by meeting qualitative and quantitative objectives. In this case, the metric for measuring performance was solely quantitative. InSound would have to achieve ambitious revenue and growth goals. While challenging to achieve, it would result in a more positive return for investors.

Earnouts can be great. They allow the seller to achieve a potentially higher return. For the buyer, it can be a relatively painless way to hedge risk and incent outstanding performance. In order to be motivating, however, the earnout must be achievable, and the incentivized party must be in a position to control its ability to achieve the objective.

At the time of Phonak's offer, InSound felt it could sell enough to achieve the earnout. They believed this because they had a third party distribution relationship with a large chain of hearing aid dispensers. This chain had recently committed to InSound a significant amount of annual minimum purchases. Given the distribution deal, David said, "I felt we had a shot. We believed the earnout was a real possibility."

After agreeing to the general terms of the acquisition, the next step was to negotiate documents. The documents turned into a long ordeal, and provided further insight into the buyer's thinking. Every issue, no matter how small, warranted a lengthy and tedious discussion. It demonstrated to InSound something was missing from this relationship. It was as if Phonak was laying traps which might inhibit InSound's success.

The negotiation came to an end and the deal closed in January 2010. David visited Phonak's company headquarters in Europe soon thereafter. On the day of his arrival, David slipped and broke his ankle. This was not a good beginning, and perhaps, a harbinger of things to come. David said, "I was injured. We had worked so hard. The negotiation was excruciating. And here I am, lying on the streets of Zurich, with a trimalleolar fracture far from home."

Soon after, David returned home for surgery and recovery. When he went back to the office, his immediate task was to develop a sales strategy for the combined company. Global sales leadership resided at corporate headquarters in Switzerland. The worldwide sales leader, in David's words, "had no idea what to do with Lyric." Phonak's senior sales management viewed the product as a risky unknown. As a result, there was no pre-vetted plan for integrating the combined salesforce or highlighting the Lyric product.

The invisible InSound device could have, and should have, been positioned for and targeted to a distinct market segment, i.e. the reluctant user, the vanity user, or the first time user. There were many choices. Positioned this way the Lyric device could fill a big gap in Phonak's product line and allow them to address that 40% of the market. In Phonak's view, however, Lyric was just another alternative available to the existing customer who was considering a hearing device from its broad line of products.

Given the centralization of sales leadership in Switzerland, and the misaligned incentives of management, InSound was essentially a distraction. David felt he had to force his way into strategic discussions to plead his case for Lyric being a critical product for the combined company. Given the misalignment of corporate sales incentives, it was soon clear that achieving the earnout was at risk.

Another curve ball came David's way after the close. Phonak had acquired a majority interest in Lyric's biggest distribution partner. InSound was anticipating significant revenues from this partner, and those revenues might be at risk. The earnout they were counting on might very well be out of reach.

For InSound, this was shocking news. It was all the more stunning because Phonak had been working on investing in this distributor while it was negotiating the acquisition of InSound. Yet none of this was disclosed in advance. Given how material this information would have been to the final deal terms, Phonak should have disclosed it to InSound. David said, "I was crushed and disappointed." For all intents and purposes, InSound had lost control over its earnout.

With the benefit of hindsight, David and his board came to realize how little they knew of their buyer. While InSound's story is extreme, the proposition stands: know your buyer. Understanding the value your company creates, for whom that value is most compelling, and how those potential acquirers operate is key to getting a great exit for your company. InSound focused on the exit late. By that time, it was too late to control its fate and do a careful vetting process. The result was an exit outcome which was lower than it might have been.

Having said all that, the story continues with a mostly positive outcome. A series of conversations took place between InSound and Phonak to address this issue. Progress was slow, tensions were mounting, and there was no visibility on a speedy resolution. To break the logjam, InSound's Chairman proposed a one-on-one discussion with Phonak's CEO at the earliest possible date.

A few days later, at the conclusion of a 5:00 AM call between InSound's Chairman and the President of Phonak, Phonak agreed to an immediate cash payment to InSound investors. This payment was essentially a purchase of the earnout. The final payment resulted in a 2.5x return to the investors on their original invested capital. While Ken Rainin and the other early investors had hoped for more, they were pleased to get a decent return.

The Lyric hearing aids continue to be available today, with many satisfied users. David Thrower, the very capable CEO, left the combined company exactly one year and one day after the acquisition of InSound by Phonak. He said, "I made a one year commitment. I fulfilled my commitment and then I was out of there." David has since gone on to lead several other startups and served on a number of corporate boards. He is a wiser man now and understands that although the Lyric was and continues to be a highly impactful and successful product, it does not mean that the company responsible for its creation was able to reap its full share of the rewards. As a growth company leader, one must think about the right potential exit partners early and often.

Chapter Twenty Two

Know and Get Known

Entrepreneur Marty Bodley understands one of the foundational rules of startup liquidity. Startups only achieve timely financial returns for their founders and investors if they are acquired, either by a corporate acquirer or by the public through an IPO. Marty also understands that the vast majority of successful startup exits are to corporate buyers. In his experience, this only happens when startups form relationships with their potential acquirers early on.

For most startups, developing relationships takes time and effort. The CEO has to make a deliberate and concerted effort to find and speak with key industry players to build rapport and awareness over time. Other startups, by contrast, are seemingly built for partnerships. These are startups focused on ecosystems, knowing they will need to work with partners to not only make their product function well but also to get it to customers. Relationship centric startups are practically prewired for potential exits. Marty Bodley's company, ZiipRoom, was one of those startups.

ZiipRoom was the result of many years of thought by Marty around the issue of the last ten feet in business communications and conferencing. In this case, the last ten feet refers to the fact that business video conferencing and screen sharing simply do not work as easily as they should. The basic long distance networking is not the problem. The problem is in the last ten feet, across that big conference table or small huddle room in every company. Conferencing equipment's usability, performance and reliability are too low for ordinary employees.

Marty's experience working for the defense contractor Raytheon and for the electronics company GN Group (the Copenhagen-based maker of Jabra headsets) introduced him firsthand to the nearly universal pain of trying to collaborate with remote colleagues, partners and prospects over video. For Marty, and everyone else in the increasingly global business environment, video conferencing tools are critical. But to everyone's frustration, they continue to be expensive, complicated, unreliable and maddening to use.

Marty stayed intrigued by this last ten feet problem. As it turned out, Marty was the perfect person to solve it. With a BSEE in Electrical and Electronics Engineering, an MSEE in Electromagnetics from the University of Massachusetts, and an executive MBA from MIT, Marty certainly had the educational chops to tackle the problem.

Marty had the experience and skills as well. After fifteen years in large enterprises, Marty combined his wireless and product management skills to become the CEO and founder of two electronic startups: Maestro, a wireless product developer and manufacturer, and Revolabs, an audio solutions provider focused on the enterprise conferencing and collaboration market. By the time Marty sold Revolabs to the Yamaha Corporation, he knew how to develop a product and bring it to market. Finding himself with some time on his hands after selling his company, Marty formed ZiipRoom and set out to solve the last ten feet problem.

Born in the midwestern suburbs of Cleveland, Ohio in the mid-1960s, Marty Bodley's childhood started out in a fairly typical middle class American way. At age eight, life took a big turn when his parents picked up the family and moved clear to the other side of the planet. As a result of that move, Marty spent three very formative years living in Australia. He said, "My parents got involved in an exchange program with the Australian government. They were both schoolteachers. Australia's population was growing and many communities needed school teachers. So I ended up as a young kid being transplanted to a new culture for three years."

The family settled in Kiama, on Australia's south east coast. Marty describes it as idyllic. He elaborates, "It was a scenic ocean town with salt breezes, scattered coastal pines along cliff tops, and some of the best beaches in the world, which included two cliffside blowholes where the surf would spray vertically up out of the rocks." Marty recalls it was the kind of small town where everybody knows everybody. "To us it was a bit of a culture shock that required some adjustment. It seemed like we had walked back in time when arriving there from the US." He continues, "If you wanted to make a phone call, there was an operator who would connect you on a switchboard." It took some time, but after a period of adjustment, the Bodleys were warmly accepted and felt at home.

Marty credits some of his success in life to the skills his Australian experience taught him: the ability to think broadly, to bridge cultural gaps and to find ways to partner with others. "I do think it shaped my character and my personality and probably my approach to business. I gained what I describe as a global perspective at an early age. When I came back from Australia, I was in fourth grade. I went back into the same elementary school I attended before I left. All my buddies were still there, and I suddenly felt like a total outlier. They had none of the perspective I did about other places, other people and other cultures."

At its core, the last ten feet problem with a video conference call is analogous to a cross-cultural problem. Every conferencing device manufacturer and software provider is its own tribe and wants to own and control its users' entire experience, end-to-end. The more the market fragmented into warring factions, the more companies were incentivized to own the entire process to give their customers any chance of a working solution. The resulting Tower of Babel stifled product effectiveness, and destroyed the user's experience. Marty said, "Our research confirmed an average of more than eight minutes of time wasted at the beginning of each meeting just getting the technology to work, often requiring costly technical support staff."

Marty's findings pinpointed a root cause. Most companies use multiple cloud services. Zoom, Skype, WebEx, Fuze, Go-To-Meeting, Join.me, Google Hangouts, Adobe Connect, AnyMeeting and UberConference all had their own tribe of loyal users. But most hardware solutions natively support only a single one, or maybe two, of these cloud video conferencing service providers. Compounding the problem, conferencing hardware generally has a poor user interface for participant authentication and for establishing connections.

Marty knew if someone could provide an easier solution they could tap into a $2.3 billion market representing 60 million conference rooms worldwide. Perhaps it was Marty's early life experience which led to his broader perspective, but when he looked at this messy market, he saw an enormous opportunity. With ZiipRoom, Marty's goal was no less than to provide universal connectivity. ZiipRoom's solution was designed to detect and automatically authenticate a participant on arrival to facilitate simple, secure wireless connectivity.

ZiipRoom's product was designed to simplify the three most common conference activities: wireless presentations, videoconferences from any video service provider, and making speakerphone calls. ZiipRoom enabled meeting room participants to wirelessly present from any device without needing to plug in a cable, make voice calls over corporate phone systems, and join video calls utilizing any video conferencing service. With ZiipRoom, things just seemed to work.

Initially, Marty expected he would need to provide a lot of the necessary hardware to make things work. He was prepared to build a basic computing device that could serve as the in-room hub for initiating calls and expected he'd probably need to create a complete kit by integrating with camera, audio and video manufacturers to provide the full functionality.

From the start, ZiipRoom was founded on the assumption it would partner with other companies for parts of its solution. And, these partners would also sell ZiipRoom's product to their customers. Marty approached the business with a philosophy of collaboration. As Marty explains it, "I would advise anyone to be very cautious about business plans that have you in a dark hole working alone for long periods of time. Of course, you have to protect your trade secrets. But there's a tradeoff, because if you don't tell people what you're doing, interesting opportunities won't come along. You won't get critical feedback, you won't pivot, and you won't make decisions that are necessary for the good of the company. You'll just keep going along down in your own underground laboratory."

Marty has a bedrock principle, "One very important concept I learned over fifteen years of being an entrepreneur is speaking with a wide audience is vital. It is important not to be overly cautious. I'm sure there are cases where people have been burned. But this idea of forming partnerships is the key to everything. Looking for win-wins along the way and doing that as much as you can is definitely a facilitator for growth, and ultimately, selling your company. A good motto to sum up my philosophy might be demo or die."

In the early days at ZiipRoom, Marty spoke to a number of potential investors. During these conversations, Marty was surprised to receive a fair amount of pushback on his desire to build a hardware device to go along with the company's software platform. Investors can be very cautious about backing hardware companies because there is a lot less room for error in hardware business plans. Compared to software companies, physical product companies have higher cost structures and lower product margins.

As it turned out, investors were not the only ones who questioned the necessity of ZiipRoom making hardware. Early in the process Marty had spoken with Logitech, one of his most likely potential partners. Logitech had just released a disruptive business conferencing device. Marty said, "It was called the Logitech Meetup. It was an all-in-one device. It was designed to be put right on top or below a display screen. It had a camera, a sound bar with speakers and a set of microphones. It was very simple to connect; an all-in-one, plug-and-play device. When they released it, they sort of dropped a bomb on the big hardware providers." But while the Logitech hardware was good, Logitech did not have the software figured out. This made them a perfect go-to-market partner for ZiipRoom.

The input from investors and Logitech got Marty thinking even more broadly about building partner relationships. What if they partnered not just for some of their hardware needs, but for ALL of their hardware needs? Rather than being a hardware competitor fighting all the other players for market share, they could live in the cloud and be the glue that tied all the balkanized hardware and software players together. This felt like the way to go. They immediately built a minimum viable product and gathered some example hardware to demo it with. They showed it to anyone who would listen: potential hardware partners, potential web conferencing partners, and potential customers.

Everyone they talked to had valuable input. Hardware players all grudgingly admitted it would make their solution more usable, and more valuable. They suggested ways ZiipRoom could improve their hardware integrations. Cloud conferencing providers saw the potential to give up having to support a huge and ever changing array of hardware configurations. They gave Marty suggestions for how ZiipRoom might work with them. Potential customers gave encouragement and vital feedback about what worked for them and what didn't, along with suggestions for how to improve the product.

Not only did all this feedback improve and speed up the product's development, it also sped up the company's path to an exit and a payout to the investors. Marty said, "I was sharing ideas, forming relationships, building partnerships, looking for win-wins along the way. Having those conversations as much as you can is definitely an accelerator for an early exit. The acquisition discussions will just start happening by default. A highly partnership driven model leads to getting on the radar of people who are looking for solutions. It's a beautiful way to do it. Imagine if you had a startup that was totally isolated and you wanted to create many excellent acquisition at bats from scratch? It would be a massive amount of work."

Marty observes it also levels the playing field by elevating the startup's credibility and perceived value. He said, "When you are in partnership mode, you are playing nice, you are in the business ecosystem, and you're having conversations with people who are potential suitors. You're not having conversations about acquisition or mergers. It's all about 'Hey I'm going to help you sell more product and you're going to help me sell more product and it's win-win and synergistic. Let's go do business together.'"

"Rather than having to walk in cold and say, 'I'd like to be acquired by you,' you get to work together, provide value and prove your worth first." Marty continues, "It's really hard to walk in with no context, and it always looks bad. Right away it's 'Why is this guy coming in to talk to me? He must be looking to try to sell his company.' Whereas with the existing partnership, the tone is all about value-add and collaboration. I'm not going in there and saying 'I want to be bought.' We never did any of that with our partners. Partnering first is much better than trying to be in the lab for three years developing something you then spring on the market. You haven't primed anybody in terms of what you're doing or let them reach their own conclusion about it. I think buyers are much more likely to buy when they think it's their idea."

Instead of focusing on being acquired, ZiipRoom went about the business of filling out its product vision and sharing it with any relevant player who would listen. Marty and his team talked to potential partners and they talked to potential enterprise customers. And as sure as day follows night, acquisition interest began to pile up. Even potential customers expressed interest in acquiring the company. Marty said, "We went into a big global co-working provider saying, 'Hey you've got tenants that want to join video calls in your meeting rooms and you don't have any technology in there. We think we have a great solution. We want you to be a customer.' They were eager to talk to us and sure enough, before long, there were M&A people showing up during our meetings."

Marty said, "We were focused on refining our minimum viable product based on the feedback we were hearing. But there were a lot of people interested in having the acquisition discussion, more so than I've ever seen. It was kind of wild." It was not limited to the obvious conference technology vendors. What really surprised Marty was the interest they drew from people adjacent to the ecosystem. Marty said, "The ultimate acquirer was not even on our radar because they were not playing in this space. We had no idea they wanted to get in. It's funny, we started gearing up to release a product and we found ourselves repeatedly having these acquisition discussions. The co-working provider was not on our list of potential acquirers, either. We knew they'd be a great customer, but we had no idea they were interested in buying technology companies. I was trying to get a great customer success story. I wanted them to be my flagship customer. And then sure enough that turned into an acquisition discussion."

As product development advanced, acquisition discussions came to a head quickly and the company ended up with three very serious potential buyers around the table at the same time. One of those buyers made an offer they could not refuse. Less than 24 months from inception, ZiipRoom was acquired by the Bose Corporation.

Because Marty understood the importance of speaking with the participants in his industry and forming win-win partnerships with key players, there was never a time when his company was not visible and relevant. As a result, he was able to drive an acquisition of the company early in its development and before he had to raise a lot of money. That fast, capital efficient outcome was good for everyone. The buyer was delighted, and the shareholders were happy with an excellent and timely return on their investment. Marty now finds himself in a job that blends the best of his enterprise and entrepreneurial experiences together. He is running a team that is helping a big company blaze a new trail in a market Marty himself was the first to recognize.

Afterword

In the Fall of 2012, Christopher and I embarked on a long term project to analyze the results from investments we made at our angel group, Launchpad Venture Group. Back then, Launchpad's portfolio of investments had resulted in slightly over twenty companies reaching some form of financial exit. About half of the exits were successes and returned more money than we invested. The other half of the exits were disappointments which returned less than the capital we invested.

We enlisted two members in our group, Ian Mashiter and Alex Brown, to work with us on this portfolio analysis research project. Ian and Alex's analytical minds helped us extract some very interesting insights during many hours of whiteboard sessions. We found a number of key trends and common themes from both our successes and failures. The end result of our research led to a new training course for our angel group members which we called *Angel 301 - Lessons Learned*.

Since the Winter of 2012, Christopher and I have taught *Angel 301* over a dozen times to Launchpad members and to investors affiliated with the Angel Capital Association. Each time we teach the class, we update our presentation with research on any new financial exits we've had over the prior months. Our course is now based on investments in over one hundred companies and has data from over fifty exits, so the number of stories we have to tell has grown quite a bit. One of the interesting patterns we noticed when teaching was the most engaging aspect of the course were the narrative examples – the stories behind the lessons. We decided that our next book would be an attempt to capture startup stories as a way of teaching their lessons.

Breaking *Angel 301* into themes and finding positive and negative examples to illustrate key points turned out to be a lot of work, but also a lot of fun. And, we added to our list of stories by bringing in Joe Mandato as a co-author. Joe's wide ranging experience working with life science companies adds an important dimension to the book.

Interviewing many entrepreneurs and capturing their stories concisely was a different kind of writing for us. We are deeply grateful to our collaborating entrepreneurs. Did we do an exhaustive job capturing every single startup lesson? Absolutely not. That was never our goal. What we tried to do was capture the themes that are amongst the most universal and consequential based on our very broad, collective experience investing over many decades. How universal are these themes? In our experience, they are issues which span many different industry verticals and business models. Every startup has a team. Every startup has to drive awareness of their product. Every startup trying to build hardware has to confront the economics of physical products. Every startup has to ride the roller coaster of timing. And every startup wishing to provide the liquidity their investors expect has to find a way to an exit for their investors.

Is there a precise science to building startups? If there is, we haven't found it. There are patterns and nearly universal rules, but like everything in life, the exception sometimes proves the rule. Are the issues in this book the only things to think about when doing your due diligence? No. Every startup is unique and the challenges of starting a company are infinitely complex and ever-changing. Are we all-knowing experts? No. One of the best things about startups is that you are always learning. But if you work around startups for long enough, you will discover these lessons are amongst the most important and most fundamental trouble spots that keep recurring. We hope you have had as much fun reading about these lessons as we had learning them.

Acknowledgements

We have many people to thank for helping us pull our research together and produce this book. First off, we have to thank Ian Mashiter and Alex Brown for their early guidance in extracting useful insights from all the data we gathered. And, we thank the many Launchpad members who sat through *Angel 301* over the years and shared their reactions, insights and questions on the materials we presented to them. Our classroom discussions and the encouragement we received is what ultimately drove us to write this book.

In addition to running Launchpad, and investing actively as individuals and fund managers, Christopher and I have written hundreds of pieces on early stage investing which we publish on *The Seraf Compass*. Over the years, we hear frequently from our audience. About two years ago, one of our readers, Becca Braun, reached out to me. Becca co-founded JumpStart Ventures, a venture development firm in Ohio, and she is actively working with business executives as they write their personal biographies and memoirs. One of her clients is Joe Mandato. As Becca said, "Joe is truly just looking to share wisdom because he loves working with young entrepreneurs and he's had so much experience – a real nuts and bolts practitioner, totally get-your-hands-dirty, let's get things done type of person."

After that type of introduction, I was eager to talk to Joe. Joe splits his time between San Francisco and Boston, so it was easy to arrange a meeting a few T stops away from where I live and work across the Charles River in Cambridge. Within minutes of meeting Joe, I knew I was speaking to a true comrade-in-arms. Although we spent our careers in different industries, lived on different coasts and invested in different innovation ecosystems, we shared a common bond in our love of the startup world and our desire to share knowledge with the next generation. Joe has an easy, infectious laugh, and I knew from early on we would enjoy working together.

From that brief introductory meeting in the summer of 2018, Christopher, Joe and I began more serious discussions about collaborating on the writing of this book. Joe brings many great stories and adds a whole new perspective to Christopher's and my writings. We are very grateful to Becca for the introduction to Joe. We are lucky to have him as a co-author for this effort. And, best of all, we had fun working on it together.

Over the past four years, Christopher and I published five books on early stage investing along with eight different training courses. Until now, the books we published were principally written as a series of educational guides for investors and entrepreneurs. Our main goal with those books was to teach versus entertain. Narrative took a back seat to teaching. We expect our readers to treat those books and course guides as desk references. With this book we strove to both entertain and teach valuable lessons. Our collective intent is to enlighten and provoke thought in an entertaining and engaging way. That's a very different writing style compared to what we typically employ. For that reason, we reached out to three experienced authors to help us meet the needs and expectations from a wider audience of readers.

Professional writer Becca Braun and *New York Times* best selling author Cheryl Richardson read early chapters of the book and gave very valuable guidance on how to best engage our readers. Writer Jay Shepherd took a critical eye to our manuscript and provided us with helpful feedback on writing style. He also forced us to address many of the issues that professional copy editors correct when they edit a book. We thank Becca, Cheryl and Jay for raising the professional standards of this book.

Hilary Bialek and Whitney Leslie are two key colleagues at Seraf. Between the two of them, they've read and edited every article, chapter and book we have written. As you can well imagine, that's a tall task. We can't thank them enough for their patience with us, and their ability to quickly turn around great feedback on the content we author. As always, we thank them profusely for editing this book. They helped keep us honest making sure we do a good job of explaining complex concepts. And they do a great job finding the tiniest of typos.

Last, but not least, we have to thank our wives, Michelle Lord and Liz Mirabile. They have been very supportive of this and all our writing. They put in significant time and effort reading the manuscript of this book and giving us their honest opinions on what they liked and disliked on our many, many drafts.

About the Authors

Ham Lord studied Computer Science at Brown University. He was involved with three software startups (MicroChem Technologies, Polygen and Advanced Visual Systems) in the early years of his career. He led software development, product management and marketing teams at these companies. The subsequent years of his career focused on investing in early stage companies. He built an angel group in Boston (Launchpad Venture Group) into the largest angel group in New England and one of the most active groups in the US. As the deal-lead on many of Launchpad's investments, he's been a board member for seven different startups over the past twenty years.

Ham first met Christopher Mirabile while running Launchpad. Christopher was starting a new phase in his career as an angel investor back in 2009. He joined Launchpad at the same time he started his own angel group called Race Point Capital. Christopher began his career in management consulting, followed by law school, and then three years as a big firm corporate attorney dedicated to working with venture backed companies and venture capital firms. For a young attorney, he participated in an incredible number of IPOs, venture financings, M&A transactions, and technology licensing deals during the wild, wild west of the early Internet Bubble years. In 1997 Christopher took a client, IONA Technologies, public on NASDAQ. Not long after, he escaped the crushing hours of his law firm and went to work in-house for IONA as their general counsel and subsequently, their CFO. After an eleven year run, Progress Software acquired IONA in 2008. After the acquisition, Christopher made the wise move and became one of Boston's most active angel investors. He is a leading voice in the local and national startup communities - speaking, teaching, advising and serving on company boards and serving as the Chair of the Angel Capital Association.

For the past ten years, Christopher and Ham worked together at Launchpad further building a large, active angel group that has invested $95 million in over 100 startup companies. In addition, to make sure they stayed humble and in touch with their entrepreneurial roots, they built their own software startup, Seraf, over the past six years. Seraf is a portfolio management solution for early stage investors. As part of creating Seraf, they launched the *Seraf Compass* as a publishing platform for all the educational content they write for early stage investors and entrepreneurs.

Joe Mandato spent the majority of his early career focused on the medical device industry. After serving four years as a Captain in the US Army Medical Services Corps, Joe left for the private sector. He was CEO of multiple companies, several of which were acquired, including Cilco AG, Ioptex Research, Origin Medsystems and Gynecare. In addition, he was a member of the founding management committee of Guidant, the medical device spin-out from Eli Lilly and led two of its five operating units. From there, Joe went into the world of venture capital and private equity. He was an Entrepreneur-In-Residence at Mayfield Fund, having served as CEO of three of its portfolio companies. In early 2003, he joined the life science-focused VC firm De Novo Ventures as a general partner and co-founder of De Novo II and III. He is now a senior advisor to the private equity firm Mainsail Partners and the wealth advisory firm Apercen Partners. Joe has invested in many early to later stage companies either as a VC or as an active angel investor. Some of his early investments in well known companies include Align Technology, Facebook and Intuitive Surgical. He has been a board member of many startup companies over the years.

Made in the USA
Middletown, DE
25 August 2020